SOFTWARE TESTING ESSENTIALS

An ISTQB® Foundation Guide

SAGAR JOSHI

Chennai • Bangalore

CLEVER FOX PUBLISHING
Chennai, India

Published by CLEVER FOX PUBLISHING 2024
Copyright © Sagar Joshi 2024

All Rights Reserved.
ISBN: 978-93-67079-21-8

This book has been published with all reasonable efforts taken to make the material error-free after the consent of the author. No part of this book shall be used, reproduced in any manner whatsoever without written permission from the author, except in the case of brief quotations embodied in critical articles and reviews.

The Author of this book is solely responsible and liable for its content including but not limited to the views, representations, descriptions, statements, information, opinions and references ["Content"]. The Content of this book shall not constitute or be construed or deemed to reflect the opinion or expression of the Publisher or Editor. Neither the Publisher nor Editor endorse or approve the Content of this book or guarantee the reliability, accuracy or completeness of the Content published herein and do not make any representations or warranties of any kind, express or implied, including but not limited to the implied warranties of merchantability, fitness for a particular purpose. The Publisher and Editor shall not be liable whatsoever for any errors, omissions, whether such errors or omissions result from negligence, accident, or any other cause or claims for loss or damages of any kind, including without limitation, indirect or consequential loss or damage arising out of use, inability to use, or about the reliability, accuracy or sufficiency of the information contained in this book.

ABOUT THIS BOOK

"Software Testing Essentials: An ISTQB® Foundation Guide" is the ideal resource for anyone seeking to understand the core principles of software testing. Whether you're a beginner building foundational knowledge or a professional aiming to deepen your expertise, this book offers the knowledge and tools you need to succeed. It is also an indispensable guide for candidates preparing for the ISTQB Foundation Level (CTFL 4.0) certification.

Carefully aligned with the official CTFL 4.0 syllabus, the book adopts a clear, comprehensive, and user-friendly approach to mastering key concepts. Complex topics are broken into digestible sections, ensuring effective learning.

Authored by Sagar Joshi for SAJO Academy Private Limited, this book simplifies even the most intricate concepts, making it practical and exam-focused. With chapter summaries, quizzes, and a full-length sample exam, readers are equipped to confidently tackle both the exam and real-world software testing challenges.

Copyright Notice:

SAJO Academy Private Limited holds full copyright over this book. Unauthorised reproduction, distribution, or use of the material is strictly prohibited, ensuring the protection of intellectual property and the book's value as a premier educational tool.

CONTENTS

About this Book .... *iii*
About the Exam .... *ix*

Chapter 1: Fundamentals of Testing 1
1.1 What is Software Testing? 3
    1.1.1 Objectives of Software Testing..8
    1.1.2 Understanding Testing and Debugging..............................11
1.2 Why is Testing Necessary? 13
    1.2.1 Testing Contributes to Success..13
    1.2.2 Testing and Quality Assurance (QA) 14
    1.2.3 Errors, Defects, Failures, and Root Causes.......................16
1.3 Testing Principles 19
1.4 Test Activities, Testware and Test Roles 22
    1.4.1 Delving into the Test Process - Test Activities and Tasks ...22
    1.4.2 Test Process in Context..25
    1.4.3 Testware 27
    1.4.4 Understanding Traceability...30
    1.4.5 Roles in Software Testing..32
1.5 Essential Skills and Good Practices in Testing...........................34
    1.5.1 Key Competencies for Effective Testing...........................34
    1.5.2 Whole Team Approach 35
    1.5.3 The Role of Independence in Effective Testing 38

Summary 42
Quiz 1 46
Quiz 1: Answers 47

Chapter 2: Testing Throughout the SDLC 49
2.1 Testing in the Context of a SDLC 51
    2.1.1 Impact of the SDLC on Testing 54
    2.1.2 Good Testing Practices in SDLC 56
    2.1.3 Testing as a Guiding Force in Software Development 56
    2.1.4 Understanding DevOps 58
    2.1.5 Shift-Left Testing Strategy 61
    2.1.6 Retrospectives: Opportunity to Inspect and Adapt 64
2.2 Test Levels and Test Types 66
    2.2.1 Test Levels 66
    2.2.2 Test Types 68
    2.2.3 Confirmation Testing and Regression Testing 70
2.3 Maintenance Testing 73
Summary 76
Quiz 2 79
Quiz 2: Answers 80

Chapter 3: Static Testing 83
3.1 Static Testing: An Overview 84
    3.1.1 Work Products That Can Be Examined 86
    3.1.2 Benefits of Static Testing 87
3.2 Feedback and Review Process 95
    3.2.1 Advantages of Early and Regular Feedback 95
    3.2.2 Review Process and Activities 96
    3.2.3 Roles and Responsibilities in Review Process 98
    3.2.4 Types of Reviews 100
    3.2.5 Factors Influencing the Success of Reviews 104

Summary 107
Quiz 3 109
Quiz 3: Answers 110

Chapter 4: Test Analysis and Design 113
4.1 Test Techniques Overview 115
4.2 Black-box Test Techniques 118
    4.2.1 Equivalence Partitioning (EP) 118
    4.2.2 Boundary Value Analysis (BVA) 120
    4.2.3 Decision Table Testing 124
    4.2.4 State Transition Testing 127
4.3 White-box Test Techniques 133
    4.3.1 Statement Testing and Coverage 133
    4.3.2 Branch Testing and Coverage 134
    4.3.3 The Value of White-box Testing 136
4.4 Experience-based Test Techniques 137
    4.4.1 Error Guessing 137
    4.4.2 Exploratory Testing 138
    4.4.3 Checklist-Based Testing 140
4.5 Collaboration-based Test Approaches 144
    4.5.1 Collaborative User Story Writing 144
    4.5.2 Acceptance Criteria 148
    4.5.3 Acceptance Test-Driven Development (ATDD) 148
Summary 150
Quiz 4 152
Quiz 4: Answers 153

Chapter 5: Managing the Testing Activities 155
5.1 Test Planning 157
    5.1.1 Purpose and Content of a Test Plan 157
    5.1.2 Planning in Agile Projects 159

    5.1.3 Entry Criteria and Exit Criteria 161
    5.1.4 Test Effort Estimations 163
    5.1.5 Test Case Prioritization 169
    5.1.6 Test Pyramid 170
    5.1.7 Testing Quadrants 173
 5.2 Risk Management 176
    5.2.1 Risk Definition and Risk Attributes 176
    5.2.2 Project Risks and Product Risks 178
    5.2.3 Product Risk Analysis 179
    5.2.4 Product Risk Control 180
 5.3 Test Monitoring, Test Control, and Test Completion 183
    5.3.1 Metrics Used in Testing 184
    5.3.2 Test Reports: Purpose, Content, and Audience 186
    5.3.3 Communicating the Status of Testing 189
 5.4 Configuration Management 191
 5.5 Defects Management 193
 Summary 196
 Quiz 5 198
 Quiz 5: Answers 199

 Chapter 6: Test Tools **203**
 6.1 Tool Support for Testing 204
 6.2 Benefits and Risks of Test Automation 206
 Summary 208
 Quiz 6 210
 Quiz 6: Answers 211

 Chapter X: Sample Exam **213**

 Chapter Y: Answers to Sample Exam **229**

ABOUT THE EXAM

Overview

The ISTQB® Certified Tester Foundation Level (CTFL) is a beginner-friendly certification for anyone interested in software testing. It covers all the key terms and concepts you must understand in Software Testing. The knowledge gained from this certificate is valuable, no matter what software development approach you use, whether it's Waterfall, Agile, DevOps, or Continuous Delivery. The CTFL certification is also required before pursuing any advanced ISTQB® certifications.

Business Outcomes

The expected business outcomes for a candidate who has achieved the new Foundation Level (CTFL 4.0) certification are:

- Understand what testing is and why it is beneficial.
- Understand the fundamental concepts of software testing.
- Identify the test approach and activities to be implemented depending on the testing context.
- Assess and improve the quality of documentation.
- Increase the effectiveness and efficiency of testing.
- Align the test process with the software development lifecycle.
- Understand test management principles.
- Write and communicate clear and understandable defect reports.

- Understand the factors that influence the priorities and efforts related to testing.
- Work as part of a cross-functional team
- Know the risks and benefits related to test automation.
- Identify essential skills required for testing.
- Understand the impact of risk on testing.

Effectively report on test progress and quality.

Exam Structure

- 40 multiple-choice questions (MCQs)
- Each question has ONE correct answer (occasionally TWO)
- Each question is worth ONE point
- No penalties for incorrect answers (no negative marking)
- 60 minutes to complete the exam (non-native English speakers get 75 minutes)
- Pass mark: 65% (26 or more points)
- The certificate is valid for life

Learning Objectives

The learning objectives are designed to support business goals and shape the Certified Tester Foundation Level (CTFL) exams.

Each chapter outlines the objectives and categorises them as follows:

- Remember (K1) – The candidate can recall, recognise, and identify terms or concepts.
- Understand (K2) – The candidate can explain reasons or give explanations for topics and can summarise, compare, classify, and provide examples of testing concepts.
- Apply (K3) – The candidate can perform a procedure for familiar tasks or choose the correct approach and apply it to a specific situation.

Chapter-wise Exam Weightage

Chapter	Chapter Name	K1 - Level	K2 - Level	K3 - Level	Total Questions	Percentage	Preparation Time (Minutes)
1	Fundamentals of Testing	2	6	0	8	20	180
2	Testing Throughout the Software Development Lifecycle	2	4	0	6	15	130
3	Static Testing	2	2	0	4	10	80
4	Test Analysis and Desing	0	6	5	11	27.5	390
5	Managing the Test Activities	1	5	3	9	22.5	335
6	Test Tools	1	1	0	2	5	20
	Total	8	24	8	40	100	1135

Official Preparation Material

The syllabus document, exam structure and rules, exam structure table, and sample exams are available for download from the official ISTQB website: https://www.istqb.org

For the ISTQB Official Glossary, visit:

https://glossary.istqb.org/en/search

Exam Tips for ISTQB Foundation Level Certification

Before the Exam:

- **Understand the Exam Structure and Rules:** Familiarise yourself with the exam format and rules, as described in this book. Knowing what to expect will help you manage your time effectively and approach the exam strategically.
- **Thoroughly Study the Syllabus:** Read the Software Testing Essentials book at least twice to ensure a solid understanding of the syllabus and key concepts.

- **Take Chapter Quizzes:** After completing each chapter, attempt the quizzes provided to reinforce your understanding and identify areas for improvement.
- **Attempt the Full-Length Sample Exam:** Use the sample exam included in this book to evaluate your preparation. Analyse your performance and revisit weaker areas to strengthen your knowledge.

During the Exam:

- **Read Questions Carefully and Completely:** Pay close attention to every word in the question. Many questions may appear to test language comprehension, so approach them patiently and carefully.
- **Be Patient and Use Your Time Wisely:** Do not rush to finish. Take your time, review your answers thoroughly, and use the entire exam duration to ensure the best possible performance.

Explore Further with SAJO Academy

To dive deeper into the concepts covered in this book, consider exploring SAJO Academy's training programmes for various ISTQB certifications.

These programmes provide:

- Comprehensive guidance on exam preparation.
- Real-world insights and hands-on exercises.
- Expert mentorship from ISTQB-accredited trainers.

Visit ***www.sajoacademy.com*** for detailed information about our courses and offerings.

Exam Registration Assistance

Need help with exam registration? We've got you covered!

As an accredited training partner with BCS, we can assist you in booking your ISTQB certification exam through BCS or the UK & Ireland Testing Board. Reach out to us via email or WhatsApp, and we'll guide you through the process and help you secure your examination at a discounted price.

Contact Us:

- Email: info@sajoacademy.com
- WhatsApp: +91 9890 674 675
- Website: www.sajoacademy.com

Let us make your exam registration smooth and hassle-free!

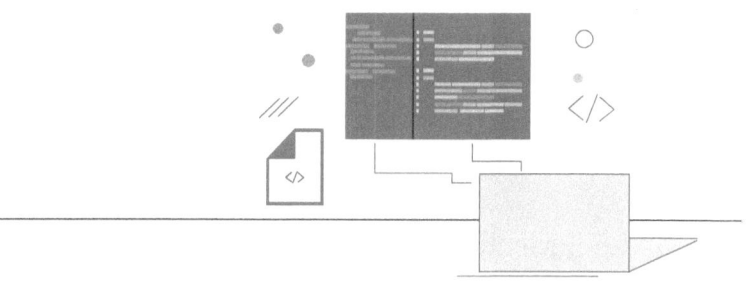

CHAPTER 1

FUNDAMENTALS OF TESTING

(8 QUESTIONS | 180 MINUTES)

Learning Objectives for Chapter 1

1.1 What is Testing?

- FL-1.1.1 (K1) Identify typical test objectives
- FL-1.1.2 (K2) Differentiate testing from debugging

1.2 Why is Testing Necessary?

- FL-1.2.1 (K2) Exemplify why testing is necessary
- FL-1.2.2 (K1) Recall the relation between testing and quality assurance
- FL-1.2.3 (K2) Distinguish between root cause, error, defect, and failure

1.3 Testing Principles

- FL-1.3.1 (K2) Explain the seven testing principles

1.4 Test Activities, Testware and Test Roles

- FL-1.4.1 (K2) Summarize the different test activities and tasks
- FL-1.4.2 (K2) Explain the impact of context on the test process
- FL-1.4.3 (K2) Differentiate the testware that supports the test activities

- FL-1.4.4 (K2) Explain the value of maintaining traceability
- FL-1.4.5 (K2) Compare the different roles in testing

1.5 Essential Skills and Good Practices in Testing

- FL-1.5.1 (K2) Give examples of the generic skills required for testing
- FL-1.5.2 (K1) Recall the advantages of the whole team approach
- FL-1.5.3 (K2) Distinguish the benefits and drawbacks of independence of testing

1.1 What is Software Testing?

Software testing is a critical process in evaluating the quality of software systems. The primary goal of software testing is to mitigate the risk of operational failures, which can have consequences ranging from financial losses and damaged reputations to severe safety hazards.

Objective: The primary aim is to assess software quality and reduce the risk of failure in real-world operations.

Activities: This involves a series of actions (processes) to identify defects and evaluate the overall quality of software products. The software/system under test (SUT) is called the "test object".

Testing is often misunderstood as merely running the software and observing outcomes. It encompasses a broader range of activities and is integral to the entire software development lifecycle. Effective testing requires careful planning, management, estimation, monitoring, and control to ensure comprehensive coverage and efficiency.

Verification and Validation

Verification: This aspect of testing verifies whether the software meets the specified requirements. For example, if a software claims to process transactions in under two seconds, verification checks this claim against actual performance.

Validation: Beyond verification, validation focuses on ensuring the software fulfils the users' and its various stakeholders' needs and expectations in its operational environment. For instance, a navigation app is validated by assessing its effectiveness in real-world travel scenarios.

Dynamic Testing and Static Testing

Dynamic Testing: This involves the actual execution of the software. It's like test-driving a car to check its performance under various conditions.

Static Testing: Unlike dynamic testing, static testing does not involve running the software. It includes methods like reviews and static analysis, like inspecting a car's design blueprints for potential issues.

While testing incorporates tools and techniques, it is predominantly an intellectual activity. Testers must possess specialised knowledge, analytical skills, and the ability to apply critical and systems thinking to identify and solve problems effectively.

The ISO/IEC/IEEE 29119-1 standard offers a comprehensive resource for those seeking an in-depth understanding of software testing concepts.

In summary, software testing is a multifaceted process beyond the mere execution of tests. It plays a pivotal role in ensuring that software systems are reliable, safe, and meet the specified requirements and the users' needs.

When Software Doesn't Work

When software doesn't work as intended, it can have serious consequences, including loss of life, money, time, and reputation. Software failures can occur in various industries, including healthcare, transportation, finance, aerospace, and many others, resulting in significant adverse impacts.

Loss of life: Software failures in critical systems such as medical devices, autonomous vehicles, or aerospace systems can result in fatal accidents or other life-threatening situations. For example, a bug in the code controlling a medical device could lead to incorrect dosages or treatment, resulting in harm or even death to patients.

Loss of money: Software failures can also result in financial losses. For example, if a financial software system fails, it can lead to incorrect calculations, data breaches, or other issues that result in economic losses for individuals, businesses, or even entire economies. Additionally, software failures may lead to costly legal battles, penalties, or fines.

Loss of time: When software doesn't work, it can significantly lose time. This includes project delays, missed deadlines, and increased system downtime, which decreases productivity and revenue. Identifying and fixing software issues may take considerable time, resulting in extended periods of disruption and inefficiency.

Loss of reputation: Software failures can damage the reputation of individuals, organisations, or products. If the software does not work as expected, it can lead to customer dissatisfaction, loss of trust, and damage to the brand image. Recovering from a damaged reputation can be challenging and may result in long-term negative consequences, such as losing customers, partners, or investors.

Therefore, ensuring software's reliability, security, and functionality is crucial to avoid these negative impacts and protect individuals' and organisations' lives, resources, and reputations. This highlights the importance of thorough testing, quality assurance, and best practices in software development and maintenance.

Software Failures Occurred in the Past

1. **Y2K Failure (Millennium Bug):** The Y2K failure, also known as the "Millennium Bug", was a notable instance of a software failure in 1999. It was a global concern that arose because older software systems used two-digit year codes to represent years, which led to the fear that when the calendar rolled over from December 31, 1999, to January 1, 2000, the systems would interpret it as January 1, 1900, instead of January 1, 2000.

   This software issue had the potential to cause significant disruptions in various industries, including finance, utilities, transportation, and more. Concerns about incorrect calculations, data corruption, system failures, and other adverse effects could have resulted in widespread failures, financial losses, and even threats to public safety.

To address this issue, extensive efforts were undertaken globally to identify and update software systems to accommodate the change in the calendar. This involved thorough testing, code remediation, and other mitigation measures to ensure the Y2K bug did not impact critical systems. Fortunately, due to the extensive preparation and remediation efforts, the actual impact of the Y2K failure was relatively minimal, with only a few localised incidents reported worldwide.

The Y2K failure is a significant example of the potential consequences of software failures and the importance of thorough testing, risk assessment, and proactive measures to mitigate risks associated with software issues.

2. **Boeing 737 Max (2019):** The Boeing 737 Max failure refers to the events that led to the worldwide grounding of the Boeing 737 Max aircraft in 2019 following two fatal crashes in Indonesia and Ethiopia. The software failure was related to the MCAS system, designed to adjust the aircraft's pitch automatically, but flaws were found in its design and functionality.

   The MCAS system relied on data from a single sensor. When the sensor provided erroneous data, it triggered repeated and aggressive nose-down adjustments, putting the aircraft into a dangerous dive. This resulted in the loss of 346 lives in the two crashes.

   The Boeing 737 Max failure had far-reaching consequences, including financial losses for Boeing, the grounding of the entire Boeing 737 Max fleet globally, negative impacts on the aviation industry, and damage to Boeing's reputation. The incident raised significant concerns about aircraft safety, regulatory oversight, and the importance of thorough testing and certification of critical software systems in the aviation industry.

As a result, extensive investigations, regulatory scrutiny, and modifications to the MCAS system and associated training procedures were undertaken to address the software failures and ensure the safe return to service of the Boeing 737 Max aircraft. The incident is a stark reminder of the criticality of software quality, safety, and regulatory compliance in developing and operating complex systems, particularly in safety-critical industries like aviation.

3. **Iridium Satellite Phone:** The Iridium satellite phone system, a global satellite-based communication network, faced challenges in customer acquisition during its initial deployment in the late 1990s. Iridium was launched as a groundbreaking technology to provide coverage of global satellite communication, including voice and data, in remote and inaccessible areas. However, despite its ambitious vision, the system struggled to acquire a sufficient customer base to sustain its operations.

Several factors contributed to the failure to acquire customers for Iridium:

High Cost: Iridium initially had high costs associated with satellite phone devices, service plans, and airtime charges, which made it relatively expensive compared to traditional cellular communication options. The high costs were a barrier to entry for potential customers, limiting the adoption of Iridium services, particularly among individual consumers.

Limited Market Demand: While Iridium offered global coverage, the demand for satellite communication services was primarily limited to specific industries and use cases, such as maritime, aviation, and remote expedition operations. The overall market demand for satellite phones was not as widespread as initially anticipated, which impacted customer acquisition efforts.

Competition: Iridium faced stiff competition from other satellite communication providers and alternative communication technologies, including cellular networks, terrestrial communication systems, and other satellite-based systems. This posed challenges in differentiating Iridium's services and capturing market share in a competitive landscape.

Technical Challenges: During its initial deployment, Iridium faced technical challenges, including satellite failures, network outages, and service disruptions. These technical issues affected the system's reliability and performance, which impacted customer trust and adoption.

Lack of Awareness and Education: As a pioneering technology, Iridium faced challenges in raising awareness and educating potential customers about the benefits and capabilities of satellite communication. Limited marketing efforts, lack of consumer understanding, and misconceptions about the technology also contributed to the failure to acquire customers.

The challenges in customer acquisition ultimately led to financial difficulties for Iridium, and the company filed for bankruptcy in 1999. However, Iridium was later acquired by a group of investors and successfully re-launched with a revised business model, targeting specific industries and use cases with more competitive pricing and improved services. Today, Iridium has a more focused customer base and continues to provide satellite communication services for various sectors, including maritime, aviation, government, and enterprise customers. The failure to acquire customers during its initial deployment is a cautionary tale about the importance of market demand, pricing, competition, technical reliability, and customer education in the success of a technology-driven business.

1.1.1 Objectives of Software Testing

The primary goals for doing software testing typically include:

1. **Assessment of Work Products:** This involves thoroughly examining various work products, such as requirements, user stories, designs, and

code, and ensuring that the user stories align with the client's needs and that the code adheres to the design specifications.

2. **Identifying Failures and Defects:** A crucial aspect is actively provoking failures to uncover defects. For example, extreme values are deliberately placed in a software application to check if it can handle unexpected scenarios.

3. **Achieving Adequate Test Coverage:** This goal ensures that all aspects of the test object are sufficiently tested, leaving no part of the software unexamined.

4. **Mitigating Risk of Poor Software Quality:** By rigorous testing, the aim is to lower the risk of releasing software that does not meet quality standards. This could involve repeated testing cycles to refine the software.

5. **Verification of Requirement Fulfilment:** This involves verifying whether the software meets the specified requirements, such as whether a feature functions as intended or meets performance benchmarks.

6. **Compliance with Legal and Regulatory Standards:** Ensuring that the software complies with relevant contractual, legal, and regulatory requirements is vital. For example, a banking application must comply with financial regulations.

7. **Informing Stakeholders:** Providing clear, comprehensive information to stakeholders to support informed decision-making. This could include reports on test results and risk assessments.

8. **Enhancing Confidence in Software Quality:** Thorough testing is key to ensuring software quality. Finding defects and failures may lower our confidence in the software, but we don't stop there. We ensure that found defects and failures are fixed before delivering the final product.

9. **Validation of Completeness and Functionality:** This involves confirming that the software is complete and functions as stakeholders expect. For example, it validates that an e-commerce website supports all the intended transaction types without errors.

Verification focuses on ensuring the product correctly implements all the specified requirements. This process involves a thorough examination, often through various testing and review methods, to provide objective evidence that the product meets all the predefined criteria and specifications. Verification is akin to asking, "Are we building the product, right?" It checks whether the product is developed correctly at each stage and aligns with the design and development documents. This step is crucial for identifying and rectifying errors early in the development cycle, enhancing the final product's quality and reliability.

Conversely, **validation** evaluates a product or system at the end of the development process to ensure it meets its stakeholders' intended use and needs. Unlike verification, which focuses on whether the product was built as per the specifications, validation is concerned with the question, "Are we building the right product?" It involves examining the final product to ascertain that it delivers the required functionality and performance in the intended environment. It effectively solves the problem or fulfils the need it was designed to address. Validation is essential as it confirms that the product is fit for purpose and meets the expectations and requirements of the end-users.

The objectives of testing can vary based on several factors, such as the nature of the work product being tested, the level of testing, the associated risks, the software development lifecycle (SDLC) model in use, and various business-related factors like corporate structure, competitive landscape, or market release timelines.

1.1.2 Understanding Testing and Debugging

Testing: In software development, testing is crucial in identifying issues. It can either lead to discovering failures due to defects (dynamic testing) or directly pinpoint defects in the software (static testing). For instance, dynamic testing might reveal a crash in an application when a specific function is used, indicating a defect. On the other hand, static testing could identify a coding error, such as a syntax mistake, without running the program. Testing is the responsibility of testers to conduct these tests and ensure the software's reliability.

Debugging: Debugging is a distinct activity primarily undertaken by developers. It involves a systematic process to address the failures identified during dynamic testing. This process includes reproducing the failure, diagnosing the issue to locate the root cause (the defect), and then rectifying this cause. For example, if a tester finds that an application crashes when processing large files, the developer's task in debugging would be to replicate this crash, find out why it's happening (perhaps a memory allocation issue), and then fix this problem. After the fix, the software undergoes confirmation testing, ideally by the same tester, to ensure the issue is resolved. Additionally, regression testing might be conducted to check if the fix has inadvertently caused problems elsewhere in the software. In contrast, when static testing reveals a defect, the debugging process is more straightforward, focusing solely on removing the defect, as there's no failure to reproduce or diagnose.

Example to understand Testing and Debugging:

Testing is the process of checking whether the calculator functions correctly. The tester inputs two numbers, 5 and 3, and presses the addition button. The test is to see if the calculator correctly displays the result, which should be 8. The tester has identified a failure if the calculator shows a different number, say 15. Testing is about determining whether there is a problem and where it might be.

Once the failure is identified (the calculator shows 15 instead of 8), the role of debugging begins. A developer performs this by examining the calculator's code to determine why it adds 5 and 3 to get 15. They might find a coding error where the program mistakenly multiples the two numbers instead of adding them. Debugging is the process of locating, analysing, and fixing the defects in the software.

1.2 Why is Testing Necessary?

Testing is a part of life. It helps ensure the product works as expected within the planned time, quality, and budget. Testing isn't just the job of the test team; everyone involved in the project can use their testing knowledge to contribute to its success. Software defects can be found and corrected earlier by testing various components, systems, and documentation.

1.2.1 Testing Contributes to Success

Testing is a cost-effective strategy for detecting software flaws. Although testing itself does not fix these defects (this is done through debugging, which is separate from testing), it is instrumental in identifying failures and defects that can be rectified, thereby indirectly enhancing the quality of the software.

Testing plays a pivotal role in assessing the quality of a software product at different stages of the Software Development Life Cycle (SDLC). These assessments are crucial for project management, aiding in vital decisions like proceeding to the next SDLC phase or making a release decision.

Moreover, testing is an indirect channel for user representation in development. By understanding and incorporating user needs, testers ensure these are reflected throughout the development lifecycle. This approach is often more feasible than involving actual users, who may be unavailable or entail high costs.

In specific scenarios, testing is mandated to fulfil contractual, legal, or regulatory standards.

Practical Examples in the SDLC

- **Requirements Reviews or User Story Refinement:** Testing involves reviewing requirements or refining user stories early in the SDLC.

This step ensures the captured requirements are correct, complete and unambiguous.
- **Evaluating System Design:** During the design phase, testing evaluates the system's architecture and design. This proactive approach helps identify potential issues before they manifest in the later stages of development.
- **Code Reviews:** Testers review code during the coding phase. With a critical mindset, testers help find defects in code more effectively. This collaboration allows for immediate feedback and quick issue resolution, enhancing the efficiency of the development process.

In summary, testing is not just about finding defects; it's a comprehensive approach to ensure software quality and project success at every stage of the SDLC.

1.2.2 Testing and Quality Assurance (QA)

It's important to distinguish between 'testing' and 'quality assurance' (QA), as they play distinct yet interconnected roles. While these terms are often used interchangeably, they represent different aspects of quality management in software projects.

1. The Role of Testing in Quality Control (QC)

Testing is a crucial component of quality control (QC), a product-focused, corrective strategy to ensure the achievement of desired quality levels in software products. QC is about identifying defects in the product and rectifying them. As a significant QC activity, testing involves formal techniques (like model checking and proof of correctness), simulation, and prototyping. For instance, in a software development project, testing might include unit tests to check individual components or integration tests to ensure that different system parts work together seamlessly.

2. Quality Assurance (QA) - A Preventive, Process-Oriented Approach

In contrast, QA is a process-oriented, preventive approach. It emphasises the importance of following effective processes to produce high-quality software. The underlying principle of QA is that a well-designed and correctly implemented process will naturally lead to a high-quality product. QA encompasses both development and testing processes and is a collective responsibility of the entire project team. For example, in QA, a software development team might adopt Agile methodologies to enhance collaboration and adaptability, improving the final product's overall process and quality.

3. Quality Management in Software Development

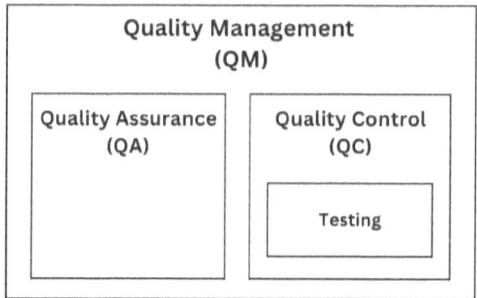

Quality Management (QM)

Quality management in software development includes both QA and QC, each with its unique focus:

- **Quality Assurance (QA):** This preventive, process-oriented approach ensures adherence to processes designed to produce quality software. It's about building confidence that the software will meet the required quality levels. The better the process, the better the software. QA applies to all stages of software development and testing.
- **Quality Control (QC):** QC is a corrective, product-oriented approach. It involves a set of activities, primarily testing, to evaluate the quality of a software component or system. QC is an integral part

of both software development and maintenance. It includes testing and other formal verification, simulation, and prototyping methods.

4. Utilization of Test Results in QA and QC

Test results play a crucial role in both QA and QC. In QC, they are used to identify and rectify defects in the software product. In QA, these results provide valuable feedback on the effectiveness of the development and testing processes. For example, many defects found during testing might indicate a need for process improvement in the development phase.

In summary, while testing and QA are related and often used in conjunction, they serve different purposes in software development's broader context of quality management. As part of QC, testing focuses on identifying and fixing product defects. In contrast, QA ensures the right processes are in place to produce a high-quality product.

1.2.3 Errors, Defects, Failures, and Root Causes

In software development, various terms describe the issues that can arise during the creation and execution of software. These terms include errors, defects, failures, and root causes. Each plays a distinct role in the software development lifecycle; understanding them is crucial.

1. **Error / Mistake:** An error, often called a mistake, is an incorrect action or decision made by a human. This could be due to time constraints, complexity, inadequate training, or simple human fatigue. For example, a programmer might mistakenly use an incorrect variable in a code or there could be a spelling mistake in the requirement text.

2. **Defect / Fault / Bug:** A defect, also known as a fault or bug, is a software flaw that will make it fail to perform its intended features or functions. It is often a direct result of an error. Defects can exist in various forms, such as errors in the code, documentation, or even

in the design of the software. For instance, a defect in a software application might be a piece of code that incorrectly calculates a value under certain conditions. If this defect is executed, it can lead to a failure.

3. **Failure:** Software failure occurs when there is a deviation from the expected performance or behaviour. It is an event that occurs when the defect gets executed. However, not all defects result in failures. Some defects may lie dormant and never cause an issue, while others may only cause failures under specific conditions. An example of a failure is a software application crashing when trying to perform a particular function due to a defect in its code.

4. **Root Cause:** The root cause is the fundamental reason behind errors or mistakes. Identifying the root cause is essential to prevent similar issues in the future. Root cause analysis involves tracing the defect back to the original error. For example, if a software failure is due to a defect in the code, the root cause might be inadequate testing procedures or a lack of proper review mechanisms in the software development process.

Here's a simple example to understand Error, Defect, Failure, and Root Cause:

- Error (Mistake): Due to fatigue, a programmer incorrectly uses the variable `totalPrice` instead of `price` in a calculation.
- Defect (Fault/Bug): This mistake leads to a defect in the software where the calculation for an invoice total is always incorrect.
- Failure: Due to this defect, when a user tries to generate an invoice, the software crashes or displays an incorrect total.
- Root Cause: The root cause is human error – the programmer's fatigue leading to the incorrect use of a variable in the code.

A thorough analysis is essential to pinpoint the root cause of defects, failures, or issues. Among the various methodologies employed for this purpose are the 5-Whys and Fishbone Analysis. The 5-Whys technique involves asking "Why?" repeatedly, usually five times, to peel back the layers of a problem and reach its core cause. This method is straightforward and effectively tracing the events leading to the issue. On the other hand, Fishbone Analysis, also known as Ishikawa or Cause and Effect Diagram, provides a more structured approach. It visually maps out different causes of a problem across various categories, like methods, machines, people, and materials, to identify potential root causes. Both methods are instrumental in critical thinking and problem-solving, enabling teams to address not just the symptoms of a problem but its fundamental source.

Example of a typical Fishbone Diagram

In summary, errors are human mistakes that lead to defects in software. These defects, in turn, can cause failures when the software does not perform as expected. Understanding and addressing the root cause of these defects is crucial in preventing future failures and ensuring the reliability and efficiency of software systems.

1.3 Testing Principles

Several guiding principles in software testing have been established over time to provide a framework for effective testing strategies. This text outlines seven fundamental principles universally applicable across various testing scenarios.

1. **Testing Identifies Defects, Not Their Absence:** Testing is a process designed to reveal the presence of defects in a software system. However, it's crucial to understand that the absence of detected defects during testing does not guarantee that the software is defect-free. For example, if software passes all its test cases, it merely indicates that the tested scenarios are free of detected issues. However, there could still be undetected defects lurking in untested areas. The Y2K defect remained unnoticed in software systems for years until it caused noticeable problems.

2. **Exhaustive Testing is Impossible:** Testing every possible scenario in a software system except in the most straightforward cases is impossible. For example, in an application with one screen containing 15 input fields, each having five possible values, testing all valid combinations would require 30,517,578,125 (5^{15}) tests, a number too high to be feasible within typical project timelines. Instead of attempting an exhaustive approach, it's more practical to employ strategic test techniques, prioritise test cases, and focus on risk-based testing. For instance, prioritising tests based on user scenarios or critical functionalities ensures that the most important aspects of the software are thoroughly examined.

3. **The Benefits of Early Testing:** Initiating testing early in the software development lifecycle can save time and money. Early detection of defects prevents the propagation of these issues into later stages, thereby reducing the overall cost of quality. For instance, identifying

a requirement flaw during the requirements analysis phase is far less costly to fix than if it were discovered post-deployment.

4. **Defect Clustering Phenomenon**: In practice, defects tend to cluster within specific components of a system. This observation aligns with the Pareto principle, where a small portion of the system might contain most issues. Recognising and focusing on these defect-prone areas, especially in risk-based testing, can lead to more efficient defect detection. For example, if a particular module has historically shown many defects, it warrants more focused testing in future iterations.

5. **The Diminishing Returns of Repeated Tests (Test wear out)**: Repeatedly conducting the same tests tends to become less effective over time in uncovering new defects, a concept known as the Pesticide Paradox. Updating test cases and introducing new ones regularly is necessary to counter this. However, in some scenarios like automated regression testing, repeated tests can be beneficial to ensure that changes haven't adversely affected existing functionalities.

6. **Contextual Nature of Testing:** Testing approaches vary significantly based on the context of the software being tested. There is no one-size-fits-all method; different software types and environments require tailored testing strategies. For example, testing a mobile application demands a different approach than trying a web-based enterprise system.

7. **The Absence-of-Errors Fallacy:** The absence of defects in a software system doesn't automatically guarantee its success or alignment with user needs. It's a common misconception that a system without defects is synonymous with success. Both verification and validation are essential; verification ensures the software functions correctly, while validation checks if it meets user requirements and business goals. For example, the software could flawlessly pass all technical tests yet fail to offer an intuitive user experience, falling short of user

expectations. This is similar to the case of the Iridium satellite phone, which, despite functioning as intended, failed commercially because it was so expensive, not aligning with what users were willing to pay. Therefore, even defect-free software might not succeed if it doesn't resonate with user needs and expectations.

In summary, these seven principles are a foundation for effective software testing, emphasising the importance of strategic, context-aware, and early testing practices to enhance software quality and functionality.

1.4 Test Activities, Testware and Test Roles

Testing is nuanced and context-dependent in software development, yet it encompasses fundamental activities crucial for meeting testing objectives. These activities collectively form what is known as the test process. This process is not static; it is dynamic and adaptable, tailored to fit the unique requirements of each project.

This section aims to demystify the general aspects of the test process, discussing in detail the various test activities and tasks, the impact of context on testing, the role and importance of testware, the traceability between test basis and testware, and the diverse roles involved in the testing process. The ISO/IEC/IEEE 29119-2 standard offers extensive insights into test processes for more in-depth exploration.

1.4.1 Delving into the Test Process - Test Activities and Tasks

The test process typically begins with careful planning and concludes with test completion activities. Each phase of this process might need repeated multiple times to meet specific exit or completion criteria. While the steps are logically sequential, they often overlap or co-occur. Key considerations in this process include determining the particular test activities, the implementation method of the test process, and the timing of these processes and activities. It's important to note that there is no universal test process; it varies based on organisational test strategies and project-specific needs.

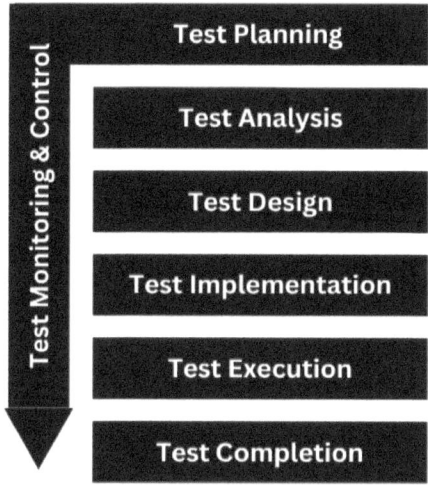

Standard Test Process

1. Test Planning

At the forefront is test planning, a phase where testing objectives are clearly defined, and an approach that best aligns with these objectives within the project constraints is selected. This phase is not just about setting goals but also about strategising the path to achieve them efficiently.

2. Test Monitoring and Control

Test Monitoring and Control are closely followed, a critical phase where the ongoing activities are continuously assessed against the plan. This phase is not just about tracking progress but also about making necessary adjustments to ensure the testing objectives are met. Thus, it acts as a compass to keep the testing process on track, much like a captain adjusting the ship's course in response to changing winds and currents.

3. Test Analysis

Test Analysis is where the team dives deep into the test basis (input to identify what and how to test, e.g., requirements, design documents, knowledge, etc.) to identify testable features and conditions. This phase is crucial as it involves evaluating the test basis and test object for potential defects, assessing their testability, and understanding the associated risks. It's a phase that answers the critical question of "what to test?" based on measurable coverage criteria.

4. Test Design

In Test Design, the focus shifts to how the testing will be conducted. It involves elaborating test conditions into test cases and other necessary testware. It's a creative phase where test cases are designed, test data requirements are defined, and the test environment is planned. As part of the test environment design, we identify the required test tools and infrastructure here. This phase addresses the "how to test?" question, laying out the blueprint for the actual testing.

5. Test Implementation

Test Implementation is where plans and designs are put into action. It includes creating or acquiring the testware necessary for test execution, such as test data, test procedures, and test scripts. This phase also involves organising these test procedures and test scripts into structured test suites and building and verifying the test environment, ensuring it is primed for practical testing. It's a phase of bringing ideas into reality.

6. Test Execution

Test execution is the action-packed phase of the testing process. It involves running the tests per the predefined schedule, whether manually or through automated means. This phase is characterised by comparing actual test results with expected outcomes, logging these results, and conducting a thorough analysis of any anomalies to understand the root causes of any deviations. Here, we document the defect reports for anomalies that do not result from test-related issues.

7. **Test Completion**

   Test completion is the reflective phase of the testing process, typically occurring at significant project milestones. It involves a comprehensive review of the testing activities, archiving valuable testware for future use, and shutting down the test environment. This phase is crucial for extracting lessons learned and identifying areas for improvement in future iterations, releases, or projects. A detailed test completion report is compiled and communicated to stakeholders, marking the closure of the testing process.

In this section, we have explored the various facets of the testing process within software development. The subsequent content will delve deeper.

1.4.2 Test Process in Context

Testing is a vital component that is seamlessly integrated into the development processes, not an isolated activity. It is essential to recognise that testing is financed by stakeholders, primarily to address their business requirements. The approach to testing is influenced by various contextual elements, which include:

1. **Stakeholders' Influence:** This encompasses their needs, expectations, requirements, and willingness to cooperate. For instance, a stakeholder prioritising rapid deployment might influence a more agile testing approach.

2. **Team Dynamics:** Team members' skills, knowledge, experience level, availability, and training needs play a crucial role. For example, a team with advanced skills in automated testing might adopt more sophisticated test automation strategies.

3. **Business Domain Considerations:** Factors such as the criticality of the test object, identified risks, market demands, and specific legal regulations are crucial. In a highly regulated industry like finance, compliance testing becomes a priority.

4. **Technical Aspects:** The type of software, its architecture, and the technology used are significant. A complex, multi-layered architecture might necessitate more rigorous integration testing.

5. **Project Constraints:** These include scope, time, budget, and resources. A project with tight deadlines might require a more streamlined testing process to meet time constraints.

6. **Organizational Context:** The organisational structure, policies, and practices are influential. A company with a culture of thorough documentation might emphasise detailed test documentation.

7. **Software Development Lifecycle (SDLC):** Engineering practices and development methods can shape the testing approach. For example, continuous testing is often integral to a DevOps environment.

8. **Tool Availability:** Tools' availability, usability, and compliance can impact testing. The choice of tools can dictate the efficiency and effectiveness of the testing process.

These factors collectively impact various aspects of testing, such as:

- **Test Strategy:** Determining the overall approach to testing, considering factors like risk and project scope.
- **Test Techniques:** Choosing specific methods for testing, like black-box or white-box testing.
- **Degree of Test Automation:** The amount of testing that should be automated depends on team skills and project needs.

- **Required Level of Coverage:** This determines how much of the software needs to be tested, which can vary depending on the application's criticality.
- **Detail of Test Documentation:** The required extent and detail of documentation are decided based on organisational and stakeholder needs.
- **Reporting:** Tailoring the reporting process to meet the needs of stakeholders and the project team.

In summary, the test process is a multifaceted aspect of software development, deeply influenced by various factors, from stakeholder needs to technical and organisational considerations. Each factor significantly shapes the testing approach, techniques, and effectiveness in meeting project and business objectives.

1.4.3 Testware

Testware encompasses a range of work products generated throughout the testing process. These products vary across organisations' creation, structure, naming, organisation, and management. Effective configuration management is crucial for maintaining consistency and integrity. Below is a non-exhaustive list of typical testware components categorised by the testing phase:

1. Test Planning:

- **Test Plan:** A comprehensive document outlining the strategy, objectives, resources, and schedule for testing.
- **Test Schedule:** A timeline detailing when each test activity will occur.
- **Risk Register:** A document listing potential risks, their likelihood, impact, and mitigation strategies.
- **Entry and Exit Criteria:** Conditions for starting and concluding test phases.

A test plan for a software application might include a risk register identifying potential security vulnerabilities, along with a detailed schedule for testing each module.

2. Test Monitoring and Control:

- **Test Progress Reports:** Regular updates on the status of testing activities.
- **Control Directives Documentation:** Records of decisions and actions to guide the testing process.
- **Risk Information:** Updated details on identified risks and their management.

In a project, test progress reports might be generated weekly to track the completion of test cases against the planned schedule.

3. Test Analysis:

- **Prioritized Test Conditions:** Specific conditions or criteria identified for testing, ranked by priority.
- **Defect Reports:** Documentation of defects found on a test basis unless fixed immediately.

Test conditions for a user interface might include checking the responsiveness of buttons and links, with high-priority conditions tested first.

4. Test Design:

- **Prioritized Test Cases:** Specific scenarios or sets of conditions to be tested, ordered by importance.
- **Test Charters:** Documents providing guidance and objectives for exploratory testing sessions.
- **Coverage Items:** Elements or aspects that need to be tested.

- **Test Data and Environment Requirements:** Specifications for the data and settings needed for testing.

A test case for an e-commerce website might involve testing the checkout process using various payment methods.

5. Test Implementation:

- **Test Procedures:** Detailed steps for executing test cases.
- **Automated Test Scripts:** Programs written to automate testing.
- **Test Suites:** Collections of test cases – test scripts and test procedures.
- **Test Execution Schedule:** Sequencing of test suites.
- **Test Data and Environment Elements:** Data and tools like stubs, drivers, simulators, and service virtualisations used in testing.

An automated script could repeatedly test a login process with different user credentials.

6. Test Execution:

- **Test Logs:** Records of test execution results.
- **Defect Reports:** Documentation of any defects encountered during testing.

Test logs for a software release might show successful tests for all features except one, which would be documented in a defect report.

7. Test Completion:

- **Test Completion Report:** A summary of the testing activities and outcomes.
- **Action Items for Improvement:** Recommendations for enhancing future projects or iterations.
- **Documented Lessons Learned:** Insights gained from the testing process.

- **Change Requests:** Suggestions for modifications, possibly as product backlog items.

The test completion report for a project might include lessons learned about the need for more thorough testing in certain areas and suggest changes for the next iteration—a change request to have additional security tests in the backlog for the next sprint.

1.4.4 Understanding Traceability

Traceability in testing refers to the systematic connection between various work products, such as test basis, test conditions, test cases, test procedures, test results, test logs, defect reports, etc. This connection is not just one-way but bi-directional, ensuring a comprehensive link throughout the test process.

Benefits of maintaining traceability:

1. **Enhancing Test Coverage Evaluation**

   A key benefit of traceability is its role in evaluating test coverage. Establishing a clear relationship between test elements and testware (like test conditions, risks, and test cases) makes it easier to measure how thoroughly testing objectives are being met.

   Example: Linking test cases directly to specific requirements ensures that each requirement is adequately tested.

2. **Risk Assessment through Traceability**

   By tracing test results to their associated risks, teams can effectively gauge the residual risk in a test object. This aspect of traceability is crucial for risk management in testing.

3. **Impact Analysis and Change Management**

   Traceability aids in understanding the impact of changes within the test process. When a change occurs, traceability helps quickly identify which parts of the test are affected.

4. **Facilitating Test Audits**

   Good traceability practices streamline the auditing process. It provides a clear trail of testing activities, making verifying compliance with IT governance criteria easier.

5. **Clarity in Reporting Communication with Stakeholders**

   Reports on test progress and completion gain clarity through traceability. By including the status of test basis elements, such as which requirements have passed or failed tests, these reports become more informative and easier to understand for non-technical stakeholders. Traceability bridges the gap between technical testing details and stakeholders' understanding. It helps present test results in a manner understandable to non-technical stakeholders.

   Example: A report might show that 70% of the requirements have passed testing, 20% have failed, and 10% are pending.

6. **Assessing Overall Quality and Progress**

   Finally, traceability provides valuable information for assessing the product's quality, the process's capability, and the project's overall progress regarding business goals.

In summary, traceability in testing is a multifaceted tool that enhances the effectiveness, clarity, and accountability of the testing process, ultimately contributing to the project's success.

1.4.5 Roles in Software Testing

This section delves into the two fundamental roles identified in software testing per the syllabus: Test Management and Testing Role. These roles are pivotal in ensuring the effectiveness and efficiency of the testing process in software development.

1. The Test Management Role

Primary Responsibilities: This role oversees the testing process, steers the team, and manages all test-related activities.

Key Activities:

- **Test Planning:** Crafting a roadmap for testing activities.
- **Test Monitoring and Control:** Keep a vigilant eye on the testing progress and make necessary adjustments.
- **Test Completion:** Ensuring all testing activities are concluded satisfactorily.

Contextual Variability: The execution of this role can vary based on the project's nature. For instance, in Agile environments, some test management responsibilities might be distributed among the Agile team members. In larger organisations, these tasks might fall under the purview of dedicated test managers.

2. The Testing Role

Primary Responsibilities: This role focuses on the technical aspects of testing.

Key Activities:

- **Test Analysis:** Evaluating testing requirements and identifying test conditions (what to test).
- **Test Design:** Develop test cases, identify required test data, and design a test environment.

- **Test Implementation:** Setting up the testing environment, writing test procedures and scripts, sequencing them into test suites and test execution schedule and preparing for execution.
- **Test Execution:** Running the tests and recording results and test logs.

Flexibility in Role Assignment: These roles are dynamic and can be assumed by different individuals depending on the project's needs. For example, a team leader, test manager, or even a development manager might take on the test management role. It's also common for one person to juggle testing and test management roles, especially in smaller teams or projects.

Factors Influencing Role Assignments

Several factors influence the allocation and execution of these roles:

- **Project and Product Context:** The nature and complexity of the project or product can dictate the extent and focus of these roles.
- **Skills of the Individuals:** The expertise and experience of the team members play a crucial role in determining how these roles are fulfilled.
- **Organizational Structure:** An organisation's structure can impact how these roles are defined and executed.

Due to limited resources, the same individual might perform both roles in a small startup working on a mobile application. In contrast, a large-scale enterprise software project might have a dedicated team for test management with clearly defined roles and responsibilities.

In summary, understanding these roles and their responsibilities, along with the factors influencing them, is crucial for the successful management and execution of the testing process in software development projects.

1.5 Essential Skills and Good Practices in Testing

1.5.1 Key Competencies for Effective Testing

Possessing specific key competencies is crucial for success in testing. These skills stem from knowledge, practice, and natural aptitude. Effective testers are skilled in their craft and excel at working collaboratively and adapting to various levels of test independence.

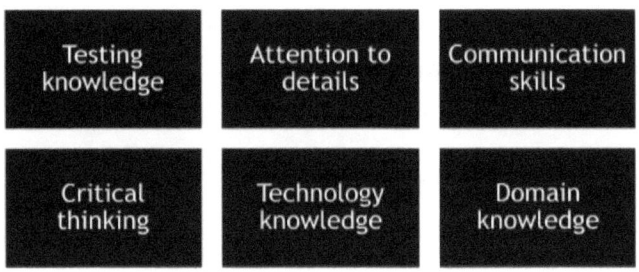

Generic Skills Required for Testing

1. **Testing Knowledge:** Mastery of testing techniques is essential for enhancing the effectiveness of the testing process. For example, understanding different testing methods, such as black-box or white-box testing, can significantly improve outcomes.

2. **Detail-Oriented Approach:** Testers must exhibit thoroughness, carefulness, and a keen eye for detail. This meticulousness is vital in uncovering hard-to-spot defects. For instance, paying close attention to minor discrepancies in software behaviour can lead to discovering critical bugs.

3. **Communication and Teamwork:** Effective communication and active listening are fundamental for testers. These skills ensure productive interactions with all project stakeholders and facilitate transparent reporting and discussion of defects. For example, a tester must effectively articulate a complex bug to developers for efficient resolution.

4. **Analytical and Critical Thinking:** The ability to think analytically and critically, coupled with creativity, significantly boosts testing effectiveness. Testers often need to think outside the box to identify potential failure points. For instance, creatively designing test cases to cover unexpected user behaviours can reveal hidden issues.

5. **Technical Proficiency:** Technical knowledge is critical to increasing testing efficiency. Utilising appropriate testing tools and technologies can streamline the testing process. For example, automated testing tools can expedite the testing cycle and improve accuracy.

6. **Domain Expertise:** Understanding the specific domain of the application under test is crucial. This knowledge enables testers to communicate better with end users and business representatives, ensuring that the software meets user needs and expectations.

It's important to note that testers often deliver unwelcome news, such as identifying defects in a product. Testers must communicate these findings constructively since this can be perceived as criticism. The goal is to present testing not as a destructive process but as a critical step towards ensuring the success and quality of the project.

1.5.2 Whole Team Approach

The Whole Team Approach is fundamental in collaborative work environments, particularly Agile software development. It emphasises the importance of every team member's contribution towards achieving collective goals. Originating from Extreme Programming, this approach values the diverse skills within a team and promotes shared responsibility for quality outcomes.

Key Aspects of the Whole Team Approach:

1. **Inclusive Participation for Project Success:** Every team member is encouraged to engage in various tasks regardless of their primary

role. This inclusive participation ensures that knowledge and skills are utilised effectively for the project's success.

2. **Shared Workspace for Enhanced Collaboration:** A common workspace, whether physical or virtual, is crucial. It fosters better communication and interaction among team members, leading to more efficient and effective collaboration.

3. **Leveraging Diverse Skills for Synergy:** The approach creates a dynamic environment where different skill sets are combined. This synergy enhances team dynamics and significantly contributes to the project's benefits.

4. **Focus on Maximizing Business Value:** This approach ensures that the project aligns closely with business objectives by involving all team members, including business representatives, in creating acceptance tests and decision-making processes.

5. **Collective Responsibility for Quality:** Quality concerns testers and the entire team. Not only testers but also developers, customers, and product owners perform testing. Most of the time, developers perform component or unit-level testing, while product owners or customers are responsible for acceptance-level testing. This collective responsibility towards quality leads to a higher standard of output and a more cohesive team effort.

6. **Knowledge Sharing and Learning:** Testers and other team members work closely, sharing insights and strategies. This collaboration not only transfers testing knowledge but also influences the overall development of the product.

In a software development team, a developer might assist in creating test cases, while a tester could provide input on user experience design. This cross-functional collaboration ensures a well-rounded product and a team knowledgeable in multiple aspects of the project.

However, it's important to note that the Whole Team Approach might not be suitable in all contexts. For example, higher test independence is often necessary to ensure unbiased and rigorous testing in safety-critical projects.

In summary, the Whole Team Approach is about breaking down silos, encouraging cross-functional collaboration, and ensuring that every team member contributes to and takes responsibility for the project's success.

The Psychology of Software Testing

The psychology of testing plays a crucial role in how you communicate and collaborate. It's essential to recognise that different objectives require distinct mindsets. Testers are often perceived as bearers of bad news, but this perspective is a fundamental aspect of their role.

Different Mindsets

1. Tester's Mindset - The Art of Destructive Thinking

- A tester must adopt a destructive mindset, which doesn't imply negativity. Instead, it involves critical thinking and a natural curiosity. For instance, a good tester might deliberately input incorrect data to see if the system can handle errors gracefully. This approach is not about finding faults for the sake of criticism but to ensure the software can withstand unexpected scenarios.

2. Developer's Mindset - The Constructive Approach

- In contrast, developers typically have a constructive mindset. They are optimistic about their code, believing in its functionality and effectiveness. While essential for creating new solutions, this optimism can sometimes overlook potential flaws. For example, a developer might focus on ensuring a feature works under normal conditions but may not consider edge cases where it could fail.

To Bridge the Gap Between These Mindsets, A Few Strategies are Essential:

- **Adopt a Fact-Based, Neutral Language:** Communication should be objective and focused on facts. Instead of saying, "Your code doesn't work," a more practical approach would be, "The code encounters an error when given this specific input."
- **Emphasize the Benefits of Testing:** Highlight how testing contributes to the overall quality of the product. For example, explain how finding and fixing bugs early in the development cycle can save time and resources later.
- **Avoid Personal Criticism:** Focus on the code and the issue, not the individual. For instance, instead of attributing a bug to a developer's oversight, discuss it as an opportunity to improve the system's robustness.

By understanding and respecting these different mindsets, testers and developers can work together more effectively, leading to higher quality software and more innovative solutions."

1.5.3 The Role of Independence in Effective Testing

The level of independence in testing can vary from having no independence to involving external independent testers. It is advantageous to incorporate multiple levels of testing, with certain stages conducted by independent testers.

I0	I1	I2	I3	I4
• Developer testing his own code	• Another developer testing code	• Independent Test Team	• User community or business representative	• Independent Testers from different Organization

Level of Independence

Developers with an independence level of I0 or I1 are encouraged to be involved in the testing process, particularly in the initial stages, like component testing. Independent test teams with an independence level of I2 or I3 perform integration and system-level tests. Acceptance testing is typically carried out by business representatives outside the development organisation, with an independence level of I4.

1. Advantages of Independent Testing

- **Enhanced Defect Detection:** Independent testing plays a crucial role in identifying defects that might be overlooked due to cognitive biases. For instance, a developer might overlook a flaw in their code due to familiarity. In contrast, an independent tester, approaching the code with a fresh perspective, is more likely to spot it.
- **Objective Feedback and Assessment:** Independent testers, free from internal politics or pressures, can provide unbiased feedback on the system. Their external viewpoint ensures a more objective assessment, which is crucial for maintaining the integrity of the testing process.
- **Validation of Assumptions and Interpretations:** Independent testers are critical in challenging and validating the assumptions made during the system's specification and implementation. For example, a developer might assume that a particular user flow is intuitive, but an independent tester might identify it as a potential user experience issue.

2. Disadvantages of Independent Testing

- **Potential for Bottlenecks:** One of the challenges with independent testing is the risk of creating bottlenecks. Separate, independent test teams might support multiple projects in the organisation. They might have their own plans and priorities and would not be able to help your project requirements, leading to delays in the testing process.
- **Reduced Sense of Quality Responsibility Among Developers:** When testing is entirely delegated to independent testers, developers might feel less accountable for the quality of their work. This detachment can impact the overall quality of the product.
- **Communication Barriers:** Physical or organisational separation between developers and independent testers can lead to communication gaps. Independent, separate test teams may not receive the correct information at the right time, which can hinder the efficiency and effectiveness of the testing process.

3. Balancing Independence in Testing

- **Tailoring Independence to Testing Needs:** The level of independence in testing should be carefully calibrated according to the type and stage of testing. For instance, developers might conduct basic tests on their code during the initial development stages. As the project progresses, peers or external testers can perform more rigorous testing, bringing different perspectives and expertise.
- **Example Scenario:** Consider a software development project. In the early stages, developers conduct unit testing to ensure individual components work as expected. As the project progresses, a separate testing team might take over for system testing, providing a fresh perspective and identifying issues developers might have missed. Finally, stakeholders or end-users might be involved in user acceptance testing, offering valuable insights from a user's perspective.

In conclusion, while independent testing offers significant benefits in objective assessment and validation, it must be balanced with effective communication and collaboration with the development team. The right level of independence, tailored to the specific testing phase and type, is crucial for the success of any testing strategy.

Summary

Understanding Software Testing:

- Software testing is essential for evaluating software quality and reducing the risk of operational failures. It involves detecting defects and assessing quality through structured actions, extending beyond mere execution to include planning, management, and oversight.
- Verification: Ensures the software meets the specified requirements.
- Validation: Confirms that the software satisfies users' needs in real-world conditions.
- Dynamic Testing: Involves executing the software to identify issues.
- Static Testing: Uses techniques like reviews and static analysis without running the software.

Key Objectives of Software Testing:

- Assessing work products such as user stories and code.
- Identify defects, ensure sufficient test coverage, and detect failures.
- Mitigating risks associated with poor software quality and verifying requirement fulfilment.
- Ensuring compliance with legal and regulatory requirements.
- Providing information to stakeholders and building confidence in software quality.
- Validating the software's functionality and completeness.

Testing and Debugging:

- Testing: Detects problems through both dynamic (revealing failures during execution) and static methods (identifying defects without execution).
- Debugging: A developer activity focused on resolving the defects and failures identified during testing. Debugging involves, reproduction of failure, diagnosis and fixing of defects.

Importance of Testing for Project Success:

- Testing plays a crucial role in quality assurance by identifying defects and supporting project management decisions.
- It contributes to project success by detecting issues early, assessing quality at various stages of the software development life cycle (SDLC), and representing the end-user's needs.

Difference Between Testing and Quality Assurance (QA):

- Testing: A quality control activity that identifies and addresses product defects.
- QA: A preventive, process-oriented approach to ensure the correct procedures for producing high-quality software.

Understanding Errors, Defects, Failures, and Root Causes:

- Errors: Human mistakes that lead to incorrect results.
- Defect / Fault / Bug: a flow in the software that makes it fail to perform its intended feature or functions.
- Failures: Occur when software behaves differently from the expected.
- Root Cause Analysis: Identifies the underlying reasons behind defects.

Testing Principles:

- Testing can reveal defects but cannot guarantee the complete absence of bugs.
- Important principles include early testing, defect clustering, and the diminishing returns of repeated tests (test wear out).
- Testing approaches should be adapted to the specific context; defect-free software does not necessarily mean successful software.

The Test Process in Software Development:

- The test process involves planning, monitoring, analysis, design, implementation, execution, and completion.

- Factors influencing the process include stakeholders, team dynamics, business domain, technical aspects, project constraints, organisational context, SDLC stage, and available tools.

Testware:

Testware encompasses various components such as test plans, progress reports, test conditions, test cases, and completion reports, all crucial for ensuring consistency and integrity in testing.

Traceability in Testing:

Traceability links test elements and testware, helping evaluate test coverage, assess risks, analyse impacts, perform test audits, clarify reporting, communicate with stakeholders, and assess overall quality.

Roles in Software Testing:

- Test Management Role: Oversees test-related activities.
- Tester Role: Focuses on technical tasks like analysis, design, implementation, and execution.
- Role assignments depend on the project or product context, team skills, and organisational structure.

Key Competencies for Effective Testing:

Essential skills include testing knowledge, attention to detail, communication, analytical thinking, technical proficiency, and domain expertise.

Whole Team Approach:

Emphasises inclusive participation, a shared workspace, synergy from diverse skills, a focus on business value, collective responsibility for quality, and knowledge sharing.

Psychology of Software Testing:

Balances the tester's critical perspective with the developer's constructive approach, emphasising objective communication and the benefits of testing.

Role of Independence in Effective Testing:

- Independent testing improves defect detection, provides objective feedback, and validates assumptions.
- Potential challenges include bottlenecks, reduced developer accountability for quality, and communication barriers.
- Effective testing requires a balance between independence and collaboration, adjusting the approach for different testing phases and types.

Quiz 1

1. A software project can succeed without any testing. (True/False)
2. The main objective of testing is to identify all defects. (True/False)
3. Software defects can arise from inadequate documentation. (True/False)
4. Testing and Quality Assurance (QA) are the same. (True/False)
5. Dynamic testing means running the software to check whether it works properly. (True/False)
6. Testing is possible even before the completion of the code. (True/False)
7. It is more effective to involve testers only after coding is finished. (True/False)
8. Testing is unaffected by timing, location, or circumstances. (True/False)
9. The later a defect is discovered, the more costly it is to fix. (True/False)
10. Involving a third-party tester is a must for every project. (True/False)

Quiz 1: Answers

1. **A software project can succeed without any testing. (False)**

   - Justification: This software will be buggy and may not meet all the requirements. Testing is crucial for ensuring the software works as intended and is free of critical bugs.

2. **The main objective of testing is to identify all defects. (False)**

   - Justification: The objective of testing is to find the defects and failures, but it is not to find ALL the defects and failures. Testing also ensures that the software meets the specified requirements and functions as expected.

3. **Software defects can arise from inadequate documentation. (True)**

   - Justification: Inadequate or incorrect documentation can lead to assumptions for the development team and testers, resulting in defects. Clear and detailed documentation is crucial for accurate development and testing.

4. **Testing and Quality Assurance (QA) are the same. (False)**

   - Justification: Testing and quality assurance are not the same but are related. Testing involves executing a system to identify bugs or defects. At the same time, QA is a broader process that includes testing and encompasses activities to improve and ensure software quality.

5. **Dynamic testing means running the software to check whether it works properly. (True)**

   - Justification: Dynamic testing refers to executing the software code to check against the requirements and ensure that the software behaves as expected.

6. **Testing is possible even before the completion of the code. (True)**

   - Justification: Static testing (such as reviews) can begin before the code is fully completed. Techniques like unit testing and test-driven development allow for early testing.

7. **It is more effective to involve testers only after coding is finished. (False)**

   - Justification: Early tester involvement will help reduce the defect and build a relationship between the development and Test teams. Early testing can identify potential issues sooner, which can be more cost-effective and efficient to resolve.

8. **Testing is unaffected by timing, location, or circumstances. (False)**

   - Justification: Testing is context-dependent. Testing activity has deadlines, test environments, etc. Testing can be significantly affected by timing, location, or circumstances, impacting the results and effectiveness of the testing process.

9. **The later a defect is discovered, the more costly it is to fix. (True)**

   - Justification: Test effort and focus are increased if defects are found later. Generally, the later a defect is discovered in the software development lifecycle, the more costly it is to fix.

10. **Involving a third-party tester is a must for every project. (False)**

    - Justification: Some projects can have small test teams within the same organisation depending on the project size. The necessity of third-party testing depends on the project's complexity, the team's expertise, and the criticality of the software.

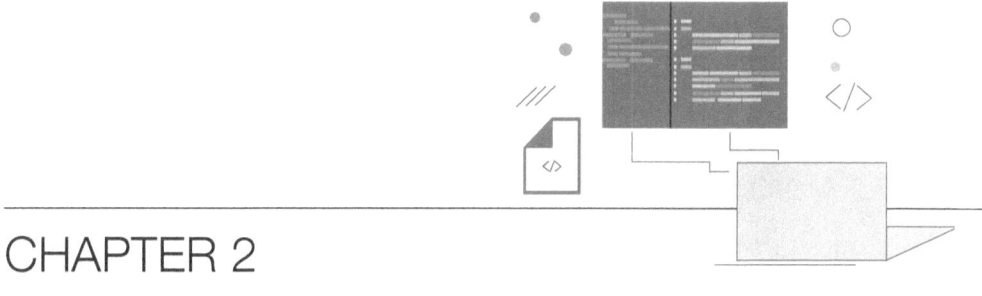

CHAPTER 2

TESTING THROUGHOUT THE SDLC

(6 QUESTIONS | 130 MINUTES)

Learning Objectives for Chapter 2

2.1 Testing in the Context of a Software Development Lifecycle

- FL-2.1.1 (K2) Explain the impact of the chosen software development lifecycle on testing
- FL-2.1.2 (K1) Recall good testing practices that apply to all software development lifecycles
- FL-2.1.3 (K1) Recall the examples of test-first approaches to development
- FL-2.1.4 (K2) Summarize how DevOps might have an impact on testing
- FL-2.1.5 (K2) Explain the shift-left approach
- FL-2.1.6 (K2) Explain how retrospectives can be used as a mechanism for process improvement

2.2 Test Levels and Test Types

- FL-2.2.1 (K2) Distinguish the different test levels
- FL-2.2.2 (K2) Distinguish the different test types

- FL-2.2.3 (K2) Distinguish confirmation testing from regression testing

2.3 Maintenance Testing

- FL-2.3.1 (K2) Summarize maintenance testing and its triggers

2.1 Testing in the Context of a SDLC

The Software Development Lifecycle model is a conceptual framework that outlines the sequence and nature of activities in a software project. It serves as a guide for organising these activities both logically and chronologically. There are various types of SDLC models, each with unique characteristics and implications for testing.

1. Sequential Development Models:

- **Waterfall Model:** This model follows a linear and sequential approach. Development activities are executed one after the other, leading to testing being conducted primarily at the end of the development cycle. Best for projects with well-defined requirements and a clear understanding of outcomes. Common in construction and manufacturing industries. For instance, the entire application would be built before significant testing begins in a project to develop a new banking application.

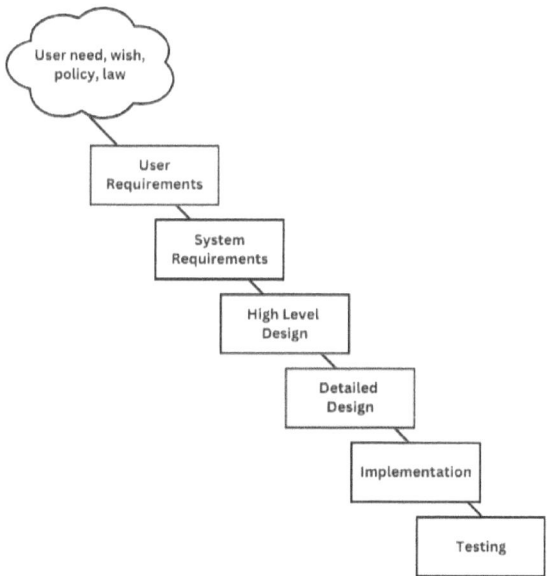

Waterfall Model

- **V-Model:** This model integrates testing more thoroughly into the development process. It aligns different levels of testing with each phase of development, promoting early testing. For example, each development phase, like requirement specification or design, would have corresponding test activities in developing a customer relationship management system.

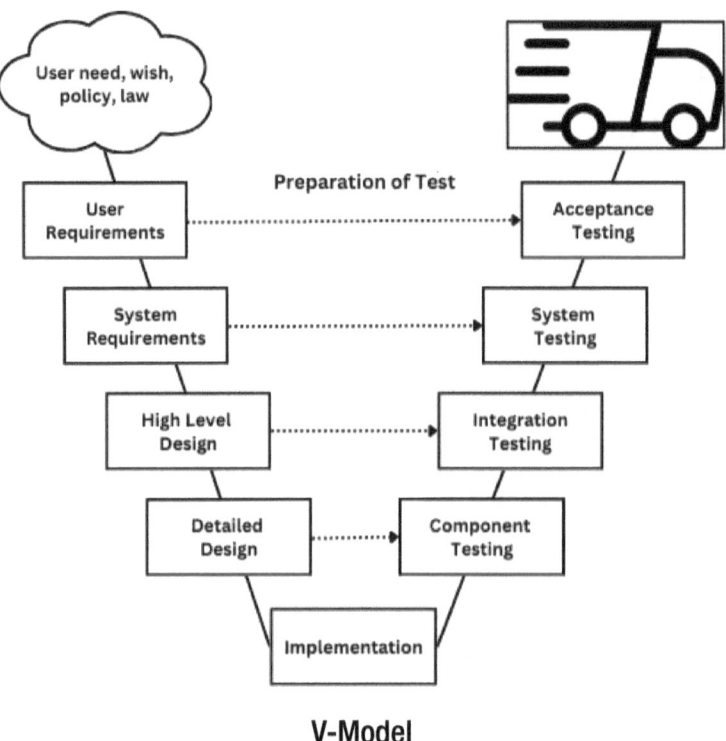

V-Model

2. Adaptive Development Models:

- **Incremental Development:** This approach involves developing and testing the system in small, manageable increments. It's beneficial when the project's requirements and solutions are well understood. Suitable for large projects where the big picture is clear, but details evolve. It is often used in software development, where the market or technology might change during development. For example, adding a new feature to an existing e-commerce platform would be done incrementally.

Incremental and Iterative Development Model
(Idea Credit: Jeff Sutherland)

- **Iterative Development:** This model systematically designs, builds, and tests feature groups. It's ideal for projects where requirements are expected to evolve, allowing for learning and adaptation. Common in new product development in rapidly changing industries. For instance, this approach might refine features based on user feedback when creating a novel mobile app.
- **Agile Development:** Agile is both iterative and incremental and is suited for complex projects. It emphasises delivering the most valuable features first. It is perfect for projects in highly dynamic environments, where speed and flexibility are crucial. Agile is widely used in software development, especially for web and mobile applications. An example is the rapid development of a software tool in a startup environment, where quick delivery and adaptability are crucial.

Selecting and Adapting SDLC Models

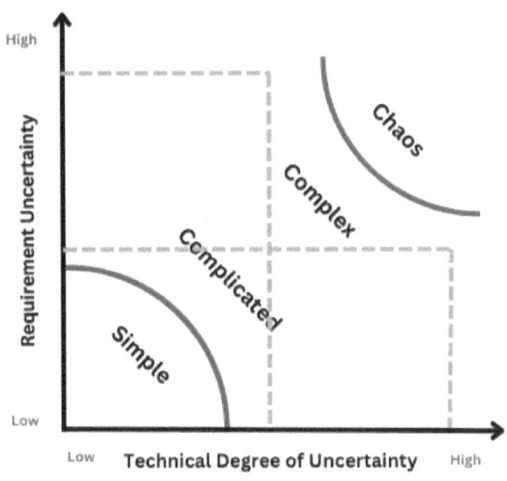

Stacy Complexity Model

The choice of an SDLC model depends on various factors, such as project goals, the type of product, business priorities, and identified risks. If the projects are simple, sequential software development lifecycles such as waterfall and V-model will work best. If the project is completed, incremental or iterative approaches are the best suited. For complex problems, Agile is the way. Chaotic projects are highly risky; we first react and then think of our actions. For example, a project with a complex product and high risk might combine sequential and agile methods to balance thorough planning with flexibility.

2.1.1 Impact of the SDLC on Testing

The success of testing in software development is closely tied to the chosen Software Development Lifecycle (SDLC) model. The SDLC significantly influences various aspects of the testing process:

1. **Scope and Timing of Test Activities:** The SDLC model determines when and how testing is conducted throughout the project. For

example, in a Waterfall model, testing activities are typically concentrated towards the end of the lifecycle. In contrast, Agile models incorporate continuous testing throughout the development process.

2. **Level of Detail in Test Documentation:** The choice of the SDLC model affects the granularity and extent of documentation required for testing. Sequential models like the waterfall often necessitate detailed test plans and upfront documentation. Agile models, on the other hand, might opt for more concise and evolving documentation to accommodate frequent changes.

3. **Choice of Test Techniques and Approach:** Different SDLC models may require different testing strategies and techniques. For instance, Agile methodologies might lean towards exploratory testing and user story-based test cases, while traditional models might use more structured test case design methods.

4. **Extent of Test Automation**: The SDLC model can influence the degree to which test automation is implemented. Agile and iterative models, which require rapid testing cycles, often benefit from more automation to ensure efficiency and effectiveness.

5. **Role and Responsibilities of a Tester:** The tester's role can vary significantly depending on the SDLC model. In Agile environments, testers often work closely with developers and participate in all stages of development. In traditional models, testers might have a more defined and separate role, focusing mainly on the testing phases.

In summary, the choice of an SDLC model has a profound impact on the testing process in software development. It shapes the scope, timing, documentation, techniques, automation, and roles within the testing phase. Understanding these impacts is crucial for tailoring the testing approach to align with the overall development strategy, ensuring both efficiency and effectiveness in delivering quality software.

2.1.2 Good Testing Practices in SDLC

Regardless of the SDLC model, certain testing practices are universally beneficial:

- **Corresponding Test Activities:** To ensure comprehensive quality control, every development activity should have a related test activity. This ensures that no aspect of the software goes untested, capturing changes that might impact functionality or performance.
- **Early and Continuous Testing:** Starting test activities early in the SDLC and aligning them with development phases enhances testing effectiveness. Testers should start test analysis and test design activities during the corresponding requirement engineering activities, not during the coding or after the development. This early involvement helps identify potential issues when they are easy and cheaper to fix.
- **Tester Involvement in Reviews:** Testers play a crucial role beyond executing tests. Testers should actively review requirements and design documents, including preliminary drafts, not just the final versions. Their involvement in the early stages of development, such as participating in code reviews, is invaluable. With their unique perspective on identifying faults, testers can pinpoint defects early in development, preventing costly fixes later.

In summary, understanding and appropriately selecting SDLC models is crucial for the success of a software project. Each model has its strengths and is suited for different types of projects. Effective testing strategies must be aligned with these models to ensure the delivery of high-quality software.

2.1.3 Testing as a Guiding Force in Software Development

In the software development landscape, three methodologies stand out for their unique approach to using testing as a primary driver for development: Test-Driven Development (TDD), Acceptance Test-Driven

Development (ATDD), and Behaviour-Driven Development (BDD). These methodologies share a common foundation in early testing and a proactive 'shift-left' approach, meaning tests are crafted before the development of the actual code. This strategy aligns well with iterative development models, enhancing the efficiency and effectiveness of the development process.

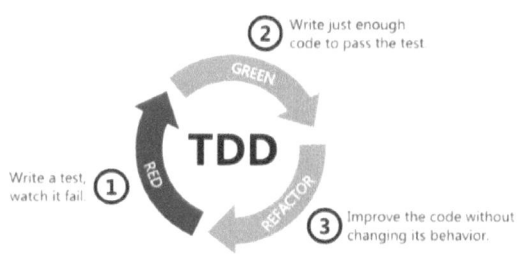

Test First Approach - TDD

1. **Test-Driven Development (TDD):**

   - **Principle:** TDD emphasises guiding the coding process through test cases. This approach often bypasses extensive upfront software design.
   - **Process:** Initially, tests are written. Following this, code is developed to meet these test requirements. Finally, the tests and the code undergo a refinement and optimisation process.
   - **Example:** Imagine writing a test for a function that calculates the sum of two numbers. The test is written first, then the function is implemented to pass this test, and finally, both are refined for better performance and readability.

2. **Acceptance Test-Driven Development (ATDD):**

   - **Principle:** ATDD focuses on deriving tests from the user stories and their acceptance criteria, which are part of the system design process.

- **Process:** Tests are formulated before the corresponding segment of the application is developed, ensuring that the development aligns with predefined acceptance criteria.
- **Example:** If the acceptance criterion is that a user interface should be user-friendly, tests are created to assess this aspect before the UI development begins.

3. **Behaviour-Driven Development (BDD):**

- **Principle:** BDD is centred around expressing an application's desired behaviour through test cases articulated in a straightforward, natural-language format.
- **Process:** These test cases, often structured in the Given/When/Then format, are converted into executable tests. This format is particularly accessible to stakeholders, facilitating better communication and understanding.
- **Example:** For a login feature, a BDD test case might be: "Given a registered user, when they enter correct login credentials, they should gain access to their dashboard."

An important aspect of all these methodologies is the longevity of tests. Tests often persist as automated checks, crucial in maintaining code quality during future adaptations or refactoring. This enduring presence of tests ensures that improvements or changes in the codebase do not compromise existing functionalities.

2.1.4 Understanding DevOps

DevOps represents an organisational strategy to close the gap between development (including testing) and operations teams. It's not just about tools and processes; it necessitates a fundamental cultural shift within the organisation. This shift is geared towards valuing development (including testing) and operations equally, fostering a collaborative environment.

Key features of DevOps include:

- **Team Autonomy:** Empowering teams to make decisions and manage their workflows independently.
- **Rapid Feedback:** Ensuring quick responses to changes or issues, enhancing overall efficiency.
- **Integrated Toolchains:** Utilizing a suite of tools that work seamlessly together, streamlining processes.
- **Technical Practices:** Embracing practices like Continuous Integration (CI) and Continuous Delivery (CD) are pivotal for rapid and reliable software delivery.

Why DevOps?

DevOps impacts the testing process in several ways. The adoption of DevOps brings several benefits, particularly from a testing standpoint:

- **Fast Feedback on Code Quality:** Quick identification of issues or potential improvements in the code. DevOps heavily relies on automation to speed up processes. Automated testing becomes a critical component, allowing for faster, more frequent, and more reliable testing.
- **Early Testing Integration (Shift-Left Approach):** This approach encourages developers to focus on quality by integrating testing early in development. In DevOps, testing is shifted left, i.e., it starts earlier in the development cycle. This approach helps identify and fix defects early, reducing the cost and time to fix them.
- **Automated Processes:** Leveraging CI/CD for efficient and consistent testing and deployment. DevOps encourages continuous integration (CI) of code, which necessitates continuous testing. This means tests are run automatically and frequently, ensuring immediate feedback on the implementation.
- **Focus on Non-Functional Quality:** Pay attention to aspects like performance and reliability, not just functional requirements. With

DevOps, performance and security testing are integrated into the development cycle rather than treated as afterthoughts. This integration ensures that applications are functionally correct but also performant and secure.
- **Reduced Regression Risk:** Extensive automated regression testing in DevOps significantly reduces the chances of new updates adversely affecting existing features. Moreover, with the accelerated pace of release cycles, testing in DevOps is strategically centred on risk management. This approach ensures that the application's most vital components are rigorously tested, diminishing the likelihood of critical failures when the software is in production.
- **Collaboration and Communication:** DevOps fosters a culture of increased collaboration between developers, testers, and operations teams. This collaboration leads to a better understanding of requirements, quicker identification of issues, and more efficient resolution of problems.
- **Monitoring and Logging:** Continuous monitoring and logging in DevOps provide real-time data that can be used for proactive testing and identifying potential issues before they become critical.

In summary, DevOps transforms testing into a more continuous, automated, collaborative, and integrated process, enhancing software development and deployment efficiency, speed and quality.

Risks and Challenges of DevOps

While DevOps offers numerous advantages, it also comes with its own set of challenges:

- **Pipeline Development:** There is a need to define and establish a robust DevOps delivery pipeline.
- **Tool Management:** Implementing and maintaining practical CI/CD tools.

- **Resource Allocation for Test Automation:** Ensuring sufficient resources are dedicated to developing and maintaining automated tests.
- **Continued Need for Manual Testing:** Despite the emphasis on automation, manual testing remains crucial, particularly for assessing the user experience.

Consider a software development team transitioning to DevOps. They start by integrating their development and operations workflows and adopting tools for CI/CD. The team begins to deploy minor, frequent updates to their application; each is automatically tested for quality and performance. While they benefit from faster deployment and reduced errors, they conduct manual user experience tests to ensure the application meets customer expectations.

DevOps is a transformative approach that aligns development and operations for more efficient and effective software delivery. It requires a cultural shift, adopting new practices, and balancing automated and manual testing to ensure functional and non-functional excellence.

2.1.5 Shift-Left Testing Strategy

The concept of initiating testing activities early in the software development life cycle (SDLC) is often termed the shift-left approach. This strategy emphasises the importance of beginning testing processes sooner rather than later, such as before the full implementation of code or the integration of various components. However, it's crucial to understand that adopting a shift-left approach does not imply ignoring testing at later stages of the SDLC.

Shift-Left – Early Testing

Key Practices for Implementing Shift-Left Testing:

1. Early Review of Specifications for Testing Purposes:

This involves scrutinising the specifications from a testing viewpoint to identify potential issues like ambiguities, gaps, or inconsistencies. For example, a team might review a feature specification to ensure all scenarios are covered and clearly defined, reducing the risk of misunderstandings during development.

2. Pre-Code Test Case Development:

Write test cases before the coding begins and execute these tests within a test harness as the code develops. If the expected result is predefined before the code is developed, it will be unbiased and more effective. For instance, a developer might write unit tests for a function before implementing it, ensuring the code meets the predefined criteria.

3. Embracing Continuous Integration (CI) and Continuous Deployment (CD):

Utilizing CI/CD practices allows for rapid feedback and the integration of automated component tests with the submitted source code in the repository. An example here would be automatically running a suite of tests every time a new code commit is made, ensuring immediate detection of integration issues.

4. **Prioritizing Static Analysis Before Dynamic Testing:**

Conducting a thorough static analysis of the source code before moving on to dynamic testing, often as part of an automated process. For instance, static analysis tools can detect potential security vulnerabilities or coding errors before executing the code.

5. **Early Non-Functional Testing:**

Starting non-functional testing, such as performance or security testing, at the component level where feasible, rather than waiting for a complete system assembly. An example could be performing load testing on individual services to ensure they meet performance benchmarks before integrating them into the more extensive system.

Benefits and Considerations:

- Implementing a shift-left approach might necessitate additional training, effort, and costs at the initial stages of the project. However, this investment is typically offset by reduced efforts and costs later in the development process due to early detection and resolution of issues.
- The success of the shift-left approach heavily relies on the buy-in and support from all stakeholders. Ensuring that everyone involved understands and is committed to this methodology is essential.

In summary, the shift-left approach in testing is a proactive strategy that involves starting testing activities early in the SDLC. It encompasses practices like early specification review, pre-code test case development, embracing CI/CD, conducting static analysis before dynamic testing, and initiating non-functional testing as early as possible. While it requires upfront investment in training and effort, the long-term benefits include enhanced efficiency and reduced costs. Stakeholder involvement and commitment are key to the successful implementation of this approach.

2.1.6 Retrospectives: Opportunity to Inspect and Adapt

Retrospectives, often termed post-project meetings, project retrospectives, or sprint retrospectives, are essential gatherings that typically occur at the end of a project, an iteration, or on reaching a release milestone or whenever necessary, depending on the Software Development Life Cycle (SDLC) model in use. Participants include testers, developers, architects, product owners, and business analysts.

The primary agenda of these retrospectives is:

1. **Continue / Keep:** Identify and discuss the successful elements of a project that should be continued.

2. **Stop:** Pinpointing areas that were less successful and needed improvement.

3. **Start:** Identify the preventive or corrective actions for the future.

The objective is to integrate these improvements and maintain successful strategies in future projects. These retrospectives must contribute to continuous improvement, and any suggested enhancements should be pursued actively.

One of the key outcomes of retrospectives is the documentation of lessons learned, particularly those relevant to testing, which are typically included in the test completion report.

The benefits of retrospectives, especially in the context of testing, are manifold:

- **Increased Test Effectiveness and Efficiency:** This is achieved by implementing process improvement suggestions from these meetings.

For example, a retrospective might reveal that automated testing tools could significantly speed up the testing process.
- **Enhanced Quality of Testware:** Jointly reviewing test processes can improve the quality of testware. For instance, a retrospective discussion might lead to the adoption of new testing frameworks that are more robust and versatile.
- **Team Bonding and Learning:** Retrospectives provide a platform for team members to raise issues and propose improvement points, fostering a learning environment. This could be as simple as sharing techniques among team members that led to successful outcomes.
- **Improved Quality of the Test Basis:** Addressing and solving deficiencies in the extent and quality of the requirements can significantly enhance the test basis. An example could be the realisation that specific user scenarios were not adequately tested, leading to a more comprehensive testing approach in future projects.
- **Better Cooperation Between Development and Testing:** Regularly reviewing and optimising collaboration can lead to more effective cooperation. An example could be the development and testing teams agreeing on a standard set of tools and communication protocols to streamline their workflow.

In summary, retrospectives are a pivotal aspect of project management and quality assurance, offering numerous benefits that extend beyond immediate project outcomes to long-term process improvements and team dynamics.

2.2 Test Levels and Test Types

2.2.1 Test Levels

Test levels in software development are set of test activities, each targeting a specific stage in the software development lifecycle (SDLC). These levels ensure software meets its requirements and functions correctly at every stage, from individual components to the complete system. The attributes of test levels include specific objectives, test basis (the reference for deriving test cases), the test object (what is being tested), typical defects and failures, and specific approaches and responsibilities.

Different Test Levels

1. **Component Testing (Unit Testing):** This level involves testing individual components in isolation, focusing on both functional aspects (like statement and decision coverage) and non-functional aspects (such as robustness and performance). It requires tools like test harnesses or unit test frameworks and is usually performed by developers in their development environments.

2. **Component Integration Testing (Unit Integration Testing):** This level tests the interfaces and interactions between components. It can be approached in various ways, such as top-down (testing from top-level components downwards), bottom-up (starting from lower-level components), functional incremental (based on functions), or big-bang (integrating all components at once).

3. **System Testing:** This level tests the entire system or product to verify that it meets specified requirements. It involves testing the overall interaction of components, including end-to-end functional testing of tasks and encompasses load, performance, reliability, and security testing. An independent test team mainly performs system testing and requires a controlled test environment.

4. **System Integration Testing:** This level focuses on the interfaces between the system under test and other systems or external services. It helps verify the seamless integration and interaction between various subsystems. Test environments that closely resemble the operational environment are crucial for this level.

5. **Acceptance Testing:** This level is about validating the system and demonstrating its readiness for deployment. It includes various forms such as user acceptance testing (UAT), operational acceptance testing, and alpha and beta testing. The intended users ideally perform acceptance testing and focus on meeting user needs.

    - **Alpha Testing:** Conducted at the developer's site by a mix of potential users and developers, it's a form of factory acceptance testing where developers observe users to identify issues.
    - **Beta Testing:** Field testing is performed at the client's location or by the end-users, providing insights into how the product performs in real-world scenarios.
    - **Operational Acceptance Testing:** This type of testing focuses on the system from an administrative perspective, covering aspects like backup and restore, installation, disaster recovery, user management, and security.
    - **Contractual and Regulatory Acceptance Testing:** Ensures compliance with contractual agreements and regulatory requirements.

Each test level is characterised by its unique objectives, test basis, test object, typical defects and failures, and specific approaches and responsibilities. This structured approach in testing ensures thorough evaluation and validation of software at each stage of its development, leading to a robust and reliable final product.

Attributes of Test Levels

Specific Objectives: Each level has distinct goals, such as verifying component functionality or assessing system integration.

Test Basis refers to the documents that derive test cases, like requirements or design specifications.

Test Object: What is being tested, whether a component, integration, system, or user acceptance?

Typical Defects and Failures: Each level targets different potential issues, from individual component bugs to system-wide failures.

Specific Approaches and Responsibilities: The methodology and responsibilities vary at each level, such as developers focusing on component testing and independent teams on system testing.

2.2.2 Test Types

This section delves into various test types that are crucial for assessing different aspects of a software system. Each test type targets specific characteristics and objectives, comprehensively evaluating the system's functionality and performance.

1. Functional Testing - Assessing "WHAT" System Does?

Functional testing is centred on evaluating the specific functions a component or system is expected to perform. This type of testing focuses on three key aspects of functional quality:

- **Completeness:** Ensuring all required functions are present.
- **Correctness:** Verifying that functions operate as intended.
- **Appropriateness:** Checking the suitability of functions for their intended use.

Functional testing is essential at all levels of testing and requires an understanding of the business problems the software aims to solve.

2. Non-functional Testing - Assessing "HOW WELL" System Performs?

Non-functional testing examines aspects other than the functional traits of a system, essentially assessing "how well" the system operates. This testing is vital across all test levels and should commence as early as possible to avoid late discovery of defects, which can be detrimental. The ISO/IEC 25010 standard categorises non-functional software quality characteristics, including:

- **Performance Efficiency:** Measures system speed and resource utilisation.
- **Compatibility:** Assesses the system's ability to function in shared environments.
- **Usability:** Evaluates user-friendliness.
- **Reliability:** Checks system consistency and availability.
- **Security:** Examines the system's defence against unauthorised access.
- **Maintainability:** Determines ease of fixing defects.
- **Portability:** Assesses the ease of transferring the system across platforms.

Non-functional testing may require specialised skills and environments, such as a usability lab.

3. Black-box Testing - Specification-Based Approach

Black-box testing, driven by specifications, involves deriving tests from external documentation. The primary goal is to verify the system's behaviour against its specified requirements. This approach measures code coverage against requirement coverage, ensuring that all specified functionalities are tested.

4. **White-box Testing - Structural Testing**

    Also known as structural or glass box testing, white-box testing bases its approach on the system's internal structure, including code, architecture, workflows, and data flows. This method requires in-depth knowledge of the system's inner workings and aims to cover various structural elements like statement, decision, and conditional coverage.

Comprehensive Testing Across Levels

Functional and non-functional testing and black-box and white-box methods are applicable at any testing level. However, the focus of these tests varies depending on the level. Various techniques derive test conditions and cases, ensuring a thorough software system evaluation.

Understanding and applying these diverse test types is crucial for comprehensively assessing a software system's functionality, performance, and reliability. Each test type offers unique insights, contributing to the overall quality and effectiveness of the software.

2.2.3 Confirmation Testing and Regression Testing
Confirmation Testing - Ensures Defect is Fixed Correctly

Confirmation testing is crucial in software development, particularly after modifications like adding new features or fixing defects. Its primary goal is to verify that the specific issue or defect initially identified has been effectively resolved. This can be achieved through the following:

1. **Re-testing with Previous Test Cases:** Implementing all the test cases that failed previously due to the defect. This ensures that the fix addresses the specific problem without introducing new issues.

2. **Introducing New Tests:** Adding fresh test cases to cover any changes made during the defect-fixing process. This helps validate the solution's effectiveness and ensures the new modifications integrate well with the existing system.

In scenarios where resources like time or budget are constrained, confirmation testing might be scaled down to more straightforward. This involves:

- **Simplified Confirmation Testing:** This involves replicating the steps that initially led to the defect and verifying that the issue no longer occurs. While less comprehensive, this approach provides a quick check to confirm that the most critical aspect of the defect has been addressed.
- **Confirmation Testing Example:** Suppose a bug was identified in a software application where a specific input caused it to crash. After fixing the bug, the same input is tested again to ensure the crash no longer occurs. Additionally, new tests are designed to check related functionalities.

Regression Testing - Maintaining Software Integrity Post-Changes

Regression testing is another essential component in software quality assurance. It comes into play after changes have been made to the software, including after confirmation testing of a fix. The focus of regression testing is to ensure that:

1. **No Adverse Side Effects:** The changes, including fixes, have not inadvertently affected other software parts. This includes checking that new defects have not been introduced or uncovered in areas of the software that remained unchanged.

2. **Comprehensive Coverage:** Conducting an impact analysis to determine the extent of regression testing needed. This analysis identifies which parts of the software might be affected by the changes, guiding the testing process to be more focused and efficient.

Regression testing is particularly suited for automation due to its repetitive nature. Automating these tests, especially in Continuous Integration (CI) and DevOps environments, enhances efficiency and ensures consistent test coverage.

Key aspects include:

- **Automating Regression Tests:** Starting automation early in the project lifecycle to build a robust suite of regression tests. This suite grows with each iteration or release.
- **Inclusion in CI/DevOps:** Integrating automated regression tests into CI pipelines, ensuring that every change is thoroughly vetted for potential regressions.

When defects are fixed or changes are made at any level of testing, it's essential to conduct both confirmation and regression testing. This dual approach ensures that the software addresses the specific issue and maintains its integrity and functionality.

Regression Testing Example: After updating a feature in a web application, regression testing is conducted to ensure that other features, like user login or data retrieval, are not negatively impacted by the update. Automated tests run through these functionalities to confirm their continued stability.

2.3 Maintenance Testing

If we are testing software or a product that is already in operation, then that testing activity is known as maintenance testing. There are various reasons why we should test an operational system. It's important to understand that maintenance testing is a testing phase, whereas maintainability is a non-functional aspect of software.

Categories of Maintenance:

1. **Corrective Maintenance:** This involves fixing defects to ensure the system operates as intended. For example, it is repairing a broken feature in a software application.

2. **Adaptive Maintenance:** This includes adding new functionalities or features to adapt to changes in the environment or user requirements. An example is updating a mobile app to support a new operating system.

3. **Performance Improvement:** This focuses on enhancing the system's performance and speeding up processing time.

4. **Maintainability Improvement:** This aims to make the system easier to maintain in the future, possibly through code refactoring or documentation improvements.

Types of Releases/Deployments:

- **Planned Releases/Deployments:** These are scheduled updates or changes made to the system, often part of a regular update cycle.
- **Unplanned Releases/Deployments (Hot Fixes):** These are urgent updates released to fix critical issues or bugs that cannot wait for the next planned release.

Testing Changes in Production:

- **Confirmation Testing:** Evaluating the successful implementation of changes to ensure they work as expected.
- **Regression Testing:** Checking for unintended side-effects in unchanged parts of the system. For instance, ensuring a new feature addition does not disrupt existing functionalities.

Impact Analysis:

- Conducted before implementing changes to assess potential consequences on other areas of the system.
- Helps decide whether the change should be made, considering the overall system integrity and deciding on the scope for testing.

Factors Influencing the Scope of Maintenance Testing:

- The degree of risk associated with the change.
- The size of the existing system.
- The magnitude of the change being implemented.

Triggers for Maintenance Testing:

1. **Modifications include** planned enhancements (like release-based updates), corrective changes, or emergency fixes such as patches for defects and vulnerabilities.

2. **Upgrades or Migrations** occur when transitioning from one platform to another, requiring testing in the new environment and for any software changes. An example is migrating a database from one server to another.

3. **Retirement:** When an application reaches its end-of-life, it may involve data migration or archiving, especially if long data retention periods are required. Testing of data restoration and retrieval procedures is crucial during this phase.

In summary, maintenance testing in operational systems is a multifaceted process that ensures the system remains functional, efficient, and relevant. It involves various types of maintenance and testing approaches, each tailored to the system's specific needs and changes. The goal is to balance introducing new features with ensuring the existing system remains stable and reliable.

Summary

Software Development Lifecycle (SDLC) Models:

- **Sequential Development Models** like the Waterfall and V-Model emphasise a linear approach, with testing often occurring at the end or alongside each development phase.
- **Adaptive Development Models** such as Incremental, Iterative, and Agile Development focus on developing and testing in small, manageable increments or cycles, suitable for evolving project requirements.

Selecting and Adapting SDLC Models:

Project goals, product type, business priorities, and risks influence the choice of an SDLC model. The model chosen significantly impacts the scope, timing, documentation, techniques, automation, and roles within the testing phase.

Good Testing Practices in SDLC: - Ensuring corresponding test activities for each development phase, early and continuous testing, and active tester involvement are key practices for effective testing across all SDLC models.

Testing as a Guiding Force in Software Development:

Methodologies like Test-Driven Development (TDD), Acceptance Test-Driven Development (ATDD), and Behaviour-Driven Development (BDD) use testing as a primary driver for development, emphasising early and proactive testing.

Understanding DevOps:

Bridging Development and Operations: - DevOps integrates development and operations, focusing on team autonomy, rapid feedback, integrated toolchains, and continuous integration and delivery. It enhances code quality, early testing integration, and automated processes and focuses on functional and non-functional quality.

Shift-Left Testing Strategy:

This approach involves starting testing activities early in the SDLC, including early review of specifications, pre-code test case development, continuous integration, and early non-functional testing.

Retrospectives:

Opportunity to Inspect and Adapt - Retrospectives involve reviewing project successes and areas for improvement, contributing to continuous improvement in testing effectiveness, efficiency, testware quality, and cooperation between development and testing teams.

Test Levels:

Organized sets of test activities targeting specific stages in the SDLC, including component testing, component integration testing, system testing, and acceptance testing, each with unique objectives and approaches.

Test Types:

Functional Testing assesses system functions, while Non-functional Testing examines aspects like performance and usability. Black-box Testing focuses on external documentation, and White-box Testing delves into the system's structure.

Confirmation Testing and Regression Testing:

Confirmation Testing ensures fixed software functions correctly, while Regression Testing maintains software integrity post-changes, ensuring no adverse side effects from updates or fixes.

Testing and Maintenance in Operational Systems:

Maintenance testing involves Corrective, Adaptive, Performance, and Maintainability improvements. It includes planned and unplanned releases/deployments and focuses on confirmation and regression testing to ensure system stability and reliability.

Quiz 2

1. Component testing is checking whether two components work correctly together. (True/False)
2. Integration testing can be done before component testing. (True/False)
3. The waterfall software development methodology is most suitable for simple projects. (True/False)
4. Retesting is an ideal candidate for test automation. (True/False)
5. The primary purpose of acceptance testing is to check whether the system can handle real-life business situations. (True/False)
6. Third-party testers must conduct the acceptance testing. (True/False)
7. Regression testing is done to verify whether the identified defects are fixed. (True/False)
8. Impact analysis is one of the main features of maintenance testing. (True/False)
9. Load testing is an example of functional testing. (True/False)

Quiz 2: Answers

1. **Component testing is checking whether two components work correctly together. (False)**

   - Justification: This is component integration testing and not component testing. Component testing, also called Unit testing, aims to check whether the component works fine independently rather than in combination with other components.

2. **Integration testing can be done before component testing. (False)**

   - Justification: Integration testing is typically done after unit/component testing. It focuses on the interaction between components, which can only be effectively tested once the individual components have been verified.

3. **The waterfall software development methodology is most suitable for simple projects. (True)**

   - Justification: The waterfall model is well-suited for projects with clear requirements and a stable scope, often found in simpler projects. Its sequential nature requires clarity on what and how tasks should be executed.

4. **Retesting is an ideal candidate for test automation. (False)**

   - Justification: Regression testing, not retesting, is more suited for test automation. Retesting is often done manually to verify specific fixes, whereas regression testing involves repetitive testing of an application.

5. **The primary purpose of acceptance testing is to check whether the system can handle real-life business situations. (True)**

   - Justification: Acceptance testing is primarily conducted to ensure that the system meets the business requirements and is ready for operational use, often involving real-life scenarios.

6. **Third-party testers must conduct the acceptance testing. (False)**

   - Justification: Acceptance testing is mainly done by the customers or end-users. Third-party testers are more commonly involved in system testing.

7. **Regression testing is done to verify whether the identified defects are fixed. (False)**

   - Justification: This is the definition of retesting. Regression testing, on the other hand, is conducted to ensure that recent changes have not adversely affected existing functionalities.

8. **Impact analysis is one of the main features of maintenance testing. (True)**

   - Justification: Impact analysis is crucial in maintenance testing as it helps identify the potential consequences of a change or what has been affected, thereby guiding the creation of compelling test cases.

9. **Load testing is an example of functional testing. (False)**

   - Justification: Load testing is a type of non-functional testing. It focuses on determining the system's behaviour under normal and anticipated peak load conditions, not the software's functionality.

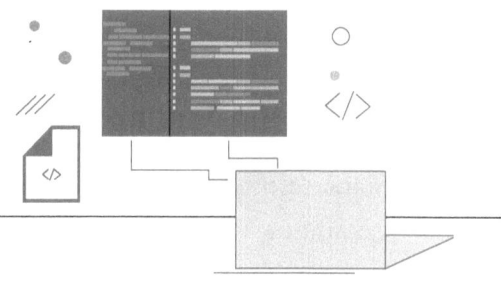

CHAPTER 3

STATIC TESTING

(4 QUESTIONS | 80 MINUTES)

Learning Objectives for Chapter 3

3.1 Static Testing Basics

- FL-3.1.1 (K1) Recognize types of products that can be examined by the different static test techniques
- FL-3.1.2 (K2) Explain the value of static testing
- FL-3.1.3 (K2) Compare and contrast static and dynamic testing

3.2 Feedback and Review Process

- FL-3.2.1 (K1) Identify the benefits of early and frequent stakeholder feedback
- FL-3.2.2 (K2) Summarize the activities of the review process
- FL-3.2.3 (K1) Recall which responsibilities are assigned to the principal roles when performing reviews
- FL-3.2.4 (K2) Compare and contrast the different review types
- FL-3.2.5 (K1) Recall the factors that contribute to a successful review

3.1 Static Testing: An Overview

Static testing is a critical process in software development that involves examining work products without executing the code. This approach is essential for verifying and validating, ensuring the software effectively meets its requirements and specifications.

Methods of Static Testing

Static testing can be conducted in two primary ways:

1. **Reviews (Manual):** This involves a thorough manual examination of various work products such as code, process documentation, requirement specifications, system architecture specifications, and testware such as test cases, test scripts, test results, and others. These reviews assess readability, completeness, correctness, testability, and consistency to improve quality and detect defects.

   A vital aspect of the review is the collaboration between testers, business representatives, and developers. This collaboration is crucial when creating collaborative user story writing and backlog refinement sessions. The goal is to ensure user stories and related work products adhere to predefined criteria, such as the Definition of Ready (DoR). Review techniques are applied to guarantee that user stories are complete, understandable, and include testable acceptance criteria.

2. **Static Analysis (Using Tools):** Tools are employed for static analysis, which helps identify potential issues in the code or other work products. This method is less labour-intensive as it does not require creating test cases.

   Static analysis offers several advantages:

- **Early Issue Detection:** It helps identify problems before dynamic testing, saving time and resources.

- **Minimal Effort Required:** Static analysis is often less effort-intensive since no test cases are needed.
- **Common in CI Frameworks**: Static analysis is frequently integrated into Continuous Integration (CI) frameworks, enhancing the overall efficiency of the development process.
- **Addresses Multiple Concerns:** It is not only used for detecting specific code defects but also evaluates maintainability and security aspects of the software.

Some of the most widely used static analysis tools include SonarQube for comprehensive code quality analysis, Fortify Static Code Analyzer for security vulnerability detection, ESLint for JavaScript linting, and Coverity for identifying defects in C, C++, Java, and other languages. These tools are renowned for their effectiveness in improving code quality and ensuring software security.

Static analysis is particularly crucial in the following:

- **Safety-Critical Systems:** Where ensuring the absence of defects is paramount.
- **Security Testing:** To identify vulnerabilities and security flaws.
- **Continuous Integration/Development:** To maintain code quality throughout the development lifecycle.

Several tools are used in static analysis, including:

- **Code Analysis Tools:** These tools scrutinise the code for potential errors and inefficiencies.
- **Spelling Checkers:** To ensure the textual content in the code and documentation is free from spelling errors.
- **Readability Tools:** These tools assess the readability of the code and documentation, ensuring they are understandable and maintainable.

In summary, static testing is a vital part of the software development process, offering a range of benefits from early defect detection to improved maintainability and security. Its collaborative nature and integration with modern development practices like CI make it an indispensable tool in the arsenal of software development teams.

3.1.1 Work Products That Can Be Examined

Static testing is a versatile technique applicable to various work products. This method is particularly effective for examining documents and code that are both readable and understandable. Key examples of such work products include:

1. **Specifications:** This encompasses business, functional, and security requirements.

2. **Product Backlog and User Stories:** Including epics, user stories, and acceptance criteria.

3. **Architectural and Design Documents:** Detailed system architecture and design specifications.

4. **Source Code:** The actual code written for the software.

5. **Testware:** This category includes test plans, test cases, test procedures, automated test scripts, and test charters.

6. **User Documentation:** Such as user guides and help documents.

7. **Web Content:** Including web pages and related digital content.

8. **Project Documentation:** Contracts, project plans, schedules, and budget plans.

9. **Infrastructure Documents:** Configuration setups and infrastructure plans.

10. **Models:** Such as activity diagrams used in Model-Based Testing, flowcharts, use-case diagrams, etc.

For effective static analysis, these work products should have a structured format. This structure could be in models, code, or text with formal syntax, allowing for a more systematic and thorough review.

However, it's important to note that not all work products are suitable for static testing. Third-party executable code, for instance, often falls outside the scope of static testing. This is primarily due to legal constraints and the inherent difficulty in interpreting such code. Static testing tools are not designed to analyse these work products, and human interpretation can be challenging.

In summary, static testing is a valuable tool for reviewing various work products in software development. By focusing on readable and structured documents, teams can effectively use static testing to improve quality and reduce errors in both documentation and code.

3.1.2 Benefits of Static Testing

1. **Early and Efficient Defect Detection:**

   Static testing is crucial for early detection of potential defects, preventing them from becoming failures. Identifying and addressing these issues in the initial stages of software development, before dynamic testing, aligns with the principle of early testing. This method allows teams to fix defects when it's easier and less costly.

2. **Low-Effort Process Without Test Cases:**

   Unlike dynamic testing, static testing doesn't require the creation and execution of test cases, making it a low-effort and time-efficient approach. This is particularly beneficial in the early stages of development when test cases might not be fully developed.

3. **Preventing Design and Coding Defects by Addressing Requirements Issues:**

   Static testing identifies defects during the requirements phase, such as inconsistencies, ambiguities, contradictions, omissions, inaccuracies, and redundancies. Early identification of these issues through reviews helps prevent potential design and coding defects, laying a stronger foundation for the development process.

4. **Detecting Defects Overlooked by Dynamic Testing:**

   Static analysis has the unique advantage of detecting defects that dynamic testing may miss. This includes unreachable code, deviations from desired design patterns, and defects in non-executable work products like documentation. This capability makes static analysis a vital complement to dynamic testing for a more thorough quality assurance approach.

5. **Seamless Integration with CI Frameworks:**

   Static analysis is often integrated into Continuous Integration (CI) frameworks, ensuring consistent code analysis and maintaining high code quality standards throughout development. This integration helps prevent defects from progressing to later stages.

6. **Boosting Development Productivity:**

   Static testing improves requirements, design, and a more maintainable codebase, enhancing development productivity. It ensures high code quality from the start, facilitating the creation of a codebase that's easier to understand, modify, and extend, thus improving maintainability.

7. **Cost and Time Reduction in Development and Testing:**

   By implementing static testing, development and testing costs, as well as the total cost of quality, are reduced. Early defect detection minimises the need for extensive fixes later, leading to a more efficient development lifecycle.

8. Enhanced Communication in Reviews:

The review process associated with static testing improves communication among team members. Requirement reviews that include diverse perspectives from developers, business analysts, marketing representatives, customers, and testers enhance understanding and collaboration, which is vital for project success.

In conclusion, static testing offers numerous benefits in software development, ranging from efficient defect detection to enhanced communication during reviews. By identifying defects early, mainly those not easily found by dynamic testing, and by improving development productivity and reducing costs, static testing is an invaluable asset in the software development process.

3.1.3 Differences between Static Testing and Dynamic Testing

Static and dynamic testing are two fundamental approaches in software testing, each playing a vital role in identifying defects in work products. While they share the common goal of defect detection, their methodologies and areas of effectiveness differ significantly.

Static Testing: Uncovering Defects Without Execution

Static testing involves examining the code without executing it. This method is particularly effective in identifying defects early in the development cycle, which can significantly reduce the cost and effort of rework. For example, a static analysis might reveal inconsistencies or ambiguities in requirements, design flaws such as inefficient database structures, or coding issues like undeclared variables. It's akin to proofreading a manuscript for errors before publishing.

Key aspects of static testing include:

- **Direct Defect Identification:** Static testing pinpoints defects directly. For instance, a code review might uncover a variable with an undefined value or duplicated code segments.
- **Applicability to Non-Executable Work Products:** Unlike dynamic testing, static testing applies to executable and non-executable work products. This includes reviewing requirement documents or design specifications for potential issues.
- **Quality Measurement of Non-Executing Code:** Static testing is instrumental in assessing qualities like maintainability, which do not depend on code execution. It ensures the code is functional, well-structured, and adherent to standards.

Dynamic Testing: Identifying Failures Through Execution

On the other hand, dynamic testing involves executing the code and observing its behaviour. This method is crucial for detecting failures that only manifest during runtime. For example, a performance test (dynamic testing) might reveal how the software behaves under load, identifying bottlenecks that were not apparent during static analysis.

Characteristics of dynamic testing include:

- **Failure Detection Leads to Defect Analysis:** Dynamic testing identifies failures and symptoms of underlying defects. Analysing these failures helps pinpoint the exact defects in the code.
- **Exclusive to Executable Work Products:** Dynamic testing applies only to executable work products, such as a compiled application or a running service.
- **Assessment of Executing Code Quality:** This measure qualities that depend on code execution, like performance efficiency. For instance, it can reveal how quickly a software application processes transactions under various conditions.

Static Testing

Here's a comparative table outlining the key differences between static and dynamic testing:

Aspect	Static Testing	Dynamic Testing
Definition	Examining the code, documents, or design without executing them.	Testing the software by running the code.
Primary Focus	Identifying defects directly in the code, design, or documents.	Identifying failures that occur during code execution.
Applicability	Both executable and non-executable work products.	Only executable work products.
Timing in Development	It can be conducted early in the development cycle.	Usually performed after a certain level of development is complete.
Defect Detection	Directly identifies potential defects.	Identifies failures, which are then analysed to find defects.
Cost of Fixing Defects	Generally lower, as defects are found early.	Potentially higher, as defects are found later in the cycle.
Quality Measurement	Non-executing code qualities (e.g., maintainability, readability).	Executing code qualities (e.g., performance efficiency, reliability).

Examples	Code reviews, static analysis tools, inspection of requirements, and design documents.	Unit tests, integration tests, performance tests, usability tests.
Benefits	Early detection of defects, reduced rework cost, and improved code quality.	Verification of functional and non-functional aspects of the software under actual conditions.

This table clearly distinguishes between static and dynamic testing, highlighting their unique characteristics and roles in software development.

In summary, static and dynamic testing are complementary techniques in the software development lifecycle. Static testing excels in early defect detection and applies to a broader range of work products, focusing on non-execution aspects like maintainability. Dynamic testing, conversely, is essential for uncovering runtime failures and assessing execution-dependent qualities like performance. Together, they form a comprehensive approach to ensuring software quality and reliability.

Typical Defects Found by Static Testing

Static testing is a critical component in the software development lifecycle, adept at identifying a wide array of defects at various stages, from initial requirements to coding and test planning. Here's an overview of the typical defects that static testing can reveal:

1. Requirements Defects

- Inconsistencies: Conflicting requirements leading to confusion in subsequent stages.

Static Testing

- Ambiguities: Vague requirements lacking clear definition and detail.
- Contradictions: Requirements that are in direct opposition to each other.
- Omissions: Essential requirements that are missing or overlooked.

2. Design Defects

- Inefficient Database Structures: Poorly structured databases can lead to performance issues.
- Poor Modularization: Lack of proper modular design, resulting in challenges in maintenance and scalability.

3. Coding Defects

- Undefined Variables: Usage of variables without proper definition.
- Undeclared Variables: Variables that are not declared with a specific type.
- Unreachable/Duplicated Code: Code segments that are either never executed or unnecessarily repeated.
- Excessive Complexity: Overly complicated code that is difficult to understand and maintain.

4. Non-compliance with Standards

- Coding Standards Violations: Code that does not adhere to established industry or organisational standards.
- Naming Convention Violations: Inconsistencies or lack of clarity in naming variables and functions, leading to confusion and potential errors.

5. Interface Specification Errors

- Mismatched Parameters: Discrepancies in the parameters expected by interfacing modules.

6. Security Vulnerabilities

- Insecure Coding Practices: Practices that potentially expose the software to security risks.
- Buffer Overflows: Vulnerabilities due to incorrect handling of data buffers.

7. Test Basis Coverage Gaps or Inaccuracies

- Missing Tests for Acceptance Criteria: Absence of tests necessary to cover specific acceptance requirements.

By identifying these defects early through static testing, teams can significantly reduce the cost and effort required for later fixes. This process ensures the software's quality, security, and reliability and contributes to a more streamlined and effective development process.

3.2 Feedback and Review Process

3.2.1 Advantages of Early and Regular Feedback

1. **Prompt Identification of Quality Issues:** Early feedback is crucial in identifying potential quality concerns. For example, if a software development team receives early input on a feature's usability issues, they can address these problems before they escalate.

2. **Consequences of Inadequate Stakeholder Engagement:** When stakeholders are not sufficiently involved during the Software Development Life Cycle (SDLC), several issues can arise:

   - **Vision Discrepancy:** The final product may diverge from what stakeholders initially envisioned or expected. Imagine a scenario where a mobile app lacks key features expected by stakeholders because their input was not sought.
   - **Failure to Meet Expectations:** This misalignment can lead to extensive rework, causing project delays. For instance, a project team might have to redo a module because it doesn't align with stakeholder expectations, leading to missed deadlines.
   - **Blame Games and Project Failure:** In extreme cases, this can escalate into blame-shifting, potentially resulting in the project's failure.

3. **Mitigating Misunderstandings with Regular Feedback:** Frequent input from stakeholders helps avoid misunderstandings regarding project requirements. For example, regular meetings with stakeholders can clarify any ambiguities in the project specifications.

4. **Timely Implementation of Requirement Changes:** With ongoing feedback, any alterations to the requirements are understood and incorporated earlier in the process. This proactive approach can be seen when a client's change in preference is quickly integrated into the project plan.

5. **Enhanced Understanding for the Development Team:** Continuous stakeholder feedback improves the development team's grasp of the project objectives. This is akin to a team gaining a clearer picture of user needs through consistent interaction with the end-users.

6. **Focusing on High-Value Features and Risk Management:** This approach allows the team to concentrate on features that offer the most value to stakeholders and effectively address identified risks. An example of this would be prioritising the development of a high-demand feature that mitigates a significant security risk.

In summary, integrating early and frequent stakeholder feedback into the SDLC is pivotal for aligning the project with stakeholder expectations, avoiding costly rework, and ensuring the delivery of a quality product that meets the envisioned requirements.

3.2.2 Review Process and Activities

The ISO/IEC 20246 standard outlines a versatile review process, offering a structured framework adaptable to various situations. This process can be customised to fit the specific needs of a review, especially in formal settings where more detailed tasks are necessary. Given the extensive size of many work products, a single review may not suffice, necessitating multiple sessions to cover the entire product thoroughly.

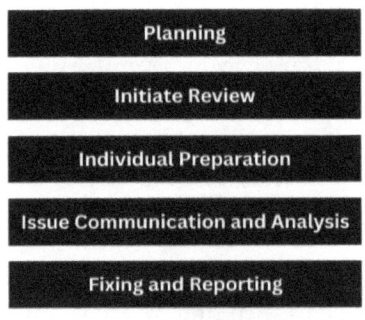

Review Process

1. **Planning:** The planning phase is crucial in setting the groundwork for the review process. It involves defining the scope of the review, which encompasses the purpose of the evaluation, the specific work product that needs to be evaluated, the quality characteristics that are of interest, and the areas that require special attention. Additionally, this phase includes establishing the exit criteria, which dictate when the review should be considered complete. Supporting information such as relevant standards, the estimated effort, and the timeframes for the review are also determined. An example could be setting a week-long timeframe to review a software module, with specific coding guidelines as the standard.

2. **Review Initiation (Kick-off):** This stage ensures that all participants are adequately prepared for the review. It involves confirming that each participant has access to the work product and understands their respective roles and responsibilities in the review process. It also includes distributing necessary materials and information to all participants, like providing a checklist for review and a design document before a design review meeting, ensuring everyone is on the same page.

3. **Individual Review:** During the individual review, each reviewer independently assesses the quality of the work product. This assessment includes identifying anomalies, making recommendations, and posing questions. Reviewers employ various techniques, such as checklist-based or scenario-based reviewing, to aid in this assessment. For instance, a checklist might be used to verify adherence to coding standards in a software review. All findings, including issues, recommendations, and queries, are recorded for further discussion.

4. **Communication and Analysis (Review Meeting):** In this phase, the anomalies identified during the individual reviews are collectively analysed and discussed. This is crucial as not all anomalies may

constitute defects. Decisions are made regarding the status, ownership, and actions required for each anomaly, typically in a review meeting. This meeting also serves to determine the overall quality of the work product and to decide on any necessary follow-up actions, including the possibility of conducting a subsequent review to ensure the completion of all actions.

5. **Fixing (Re-work) and Reporting:** The final phase involves creating detailed reports for each identified defect to facilitate tracking of corrective actions. The review process is deemed complete once the predefined exit criteria are met, leading to the acceptance of the work product. The outcomes and findings of the review process are then formally reported, which might include presenting a summary report to stakeholders that outlines the review process and its results.

3.2.3 Roles and Responsibilities in Review Process

In review processes, various stakeholders assume distinct roles, each with responsibilities. Understanding these roles is crucial for the smooth execution of reviews. Below is a detailed breakdown of these roles:

1. **Manager**
- The manager is responsible for decisions on the reviews. This includes deciding what artefacts will be reviewed and with what type of review.
- They allocate necessary resources such as staff and time, ensuring the review process is adequately supported.
- The manager also monitors the cost-effectiveness of the review process and implements control actions as needed.

2. **Moderator (Facilitator)**
- The moderator is key to the effective running of review meetings. They ensure that the sessions proceed smoothly and efficiently.

- Responsibilities include mediation between different stakeholders, managing the time during meetings, and ensuring a safe environment where all participants feel comfortable to speak freely.

The success of the review is dependent on the moderator.

3. Review Leader

- The review leader has overall responsibility for the entire review process.
- They make critical decisions about who will be involved in the review and organise the logistics, such as scheduling the meeting and deciding when and where it should occur.
- Follow up on the rework and ensure the review is completed within the defined timeline.

4. Reviewer

- Reviewers are individuals with specific technical or business expertise relevant to the review subject.
- Their main task is identifying anomalies, describing their findings, and contributing their expertise to the review process.
- Findings could be actual defects, recommendations, or even questions.

5. Author

- The author is responsible for creating the work product under review.
- If necessary, they also address and fix defects (re-work) in the work product based on findings from the review.

6. Scribe (Recorder)

- The scribe documents all anomalies, decisions, and other important information during the review.
- This role is crucial for maintaining a clear record of the review process and its outcomes.

It's important to note that one person may play multiple roles in a review process. For instance, a review leader might also be a reviewer, or an author might take on the role of a scribe. For another example, in a review of a test plan document, the manager who created the document acts as the author. In such cases, individuals must fully embrace each role's responsibilities. However, keeping the moderator role independent is generally advisable to avoid conflicts of interest.

The flexibility of role assignment allows for adaptability in different review scenarios, as outlined in the ISO/IEC 20246 standard. However, it's crucial for the effectiveness and integrity of the review process that each role is clearly defined and its responsibilities are well understood and executed by the stakeholders involved.

3.2.4 Types of Reviews

In software development, reviews are crucial in ensuring the quality and effectiveness of work products. These reviews vary widely, from informal to formal, and are chosen based on several key factors.

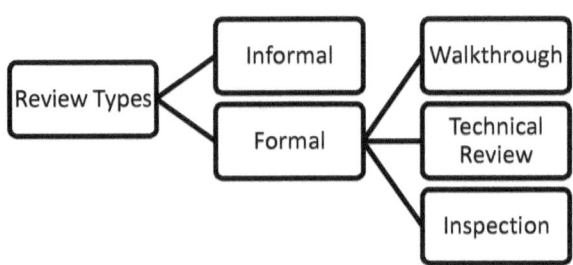

Review Types

Factors Influencing Review Type Selection:

- Software Development Life Cycle (SDLC) adherence
- Maturity of the development process

- Criticality and complexity of the product
- Legal and regulatory requirements
- Necessity for an audit trail

A single work product might undergo multiple reviews, starting from an informal review and progressing to more formal methods.

Choosing the Right Review Type:

The selection of a review type is vital for meeting specific review goals. This decision is influenced by:

- Project requirements
- Available resources
- Type and risks associated with the work product
- Business domain
- Organizational culture

Review Types:

1. Informal Reviews:

Informal reviews are characterised by their lack of a defined process and formal documentation. The primary objective of these reviews is the detection of anomalies. An example of an informal review is pair programming, where two individuals collaboratively examine designs and code unscripted and spontaneously. Another instance could involve requesting a colleague to review an email you've drafted for communication with a customer. This type of review is widely regarded as valuable and cost-effective due to its flexibility and ease of implementation.

2. Formal Reviews:

In contrast, formal reviews are characterised by strict adherence to documented procedures and specific requirements. Within the formal reviews, various forms are employed, including Walkthroughs, Technical

Reviews, and Inspections, each serving unique purposes. The level of formality increases as we move from Walkthroughs to Technical Reviews and finally to Inspections. Walkthroughs tend to be less formal, Technical Reviews exhibit moderate formality, and Inspections are the most formal.

a. Walkthrough:

A Walkthrough is a step-by-step presentation led by the author of the work product. Its purposes are multifaceted, including evaluating quality, building confidence in the work product, educating reviewers, gaining consensus, generating new ideas, motivating authors, and detecting anomalies. While individual reviews before the walkthrough and the use of checklists are optional, they can enhance the effectiveness of the process.

Walkthrough reviews are particularly effective when examining a Proof of Concept (PoC) or a design document. In this type of review, the author can present their concept, allowing participants to offer suggestions and propose alternative approaches based on their experiences. This collaborative process enriches the discussion and provides a valuable learning opportunity for the author and the participants. Scribe is mandatory for a walkthrough type of review.

b. Technical Review:

Technical Reviews involve peers and technical experts, with no participation from management. These reviews aim to gain consensus on technical issues, detect anomalies, evaluate quality, generate new ideas, and motivate authors to improve. Essential components of a technical review include individual preparation, defect logs, and review reports, with optional elements like review meetings, a trained moderator, and checklists.

These reviews are particularly effective when reviewing technical documents like test cases or test scripts. In such scenarios, involving just one peer for the review might be sufficient. This focused approach allows for a detailed and specialised examination of technical content, ensuring that the review is thorough and relevant to the specific technical aspects of the project. Scribe is mandatory for a technical review.

c. Inspection:

Inspections represent the most formal type of review. They follow a complete review process, requiring individual preparation, the use of entry and exit criteria, defined roles, and checklists. The review meeting in an inspection is led by a trained facilitator, not the work product's author. The author also cannot serve as the review leader or scribe. The objectives of inspections are comprehensive, aiming to find the maximum number of anomalies, evaluate quality, and motivate authors to improve. An essential aspect of inspections is the collection and utilisation of metrics to enhance the SDLC and the inspection process.

Inspections are adequate for reviewing documents such as test plans requiring formal approval. They are also well-suited for examining materials of critical or crucial importance. Inspections are often preferred in scenarios where safety-relevant requirements are under review due to their thorough and formal nature. This approach ensures that such vital elements are scrutinised with the utmost attention to detail and rigour, facilitating a comprehensive and reliable evaluation.

In summary, the selection and execution of the appropriate review type are pivotal in the software development process. Each type, from informal reviews to formal inspections, serves specific purposes and contributes uniquely to the overall quality and success of the software product.

3.2.5 Factors Influencing the Success of Reviews

Various critical factors influence the success of reviews in a software development context. These factors encompass both the procedural aspects of the review process and the psychological aspects that contribute to a positive and productive review environment.

Key Success Factors for Reviews:

1. **Clear Objectives and Measurable Exit Criteria**

   - Defining clear objectives and establishing measurable exit criteria are essential to guide the review process effectively.
   - Example: In a code review, a clear objective might be to identify and rectify coding standards violations, and an exit criterion could be the resolution of 90% of identified issues.

2. **Appropriate Review Type Selection**

   - Choosing the right review type is vital. It should align with the specific objectives, the nature of the work product, the participants involved, and the project's unique requirements.
   - Example: A design document may benefit from a Walkthrough review type where the author presents their concept, allowing participants to suggest alternatives based on their expertise.

3. **Chunked Reviews to Maintain Concentration**

   - Reviews should be conducted on smaller, manageable portions of work products. This prevents reviewers from losing focus during individual reviews and review meetings.
   - Example: Rather than reviewing an entire 100-page document in one sitting, break it down into chapters or sections for more effective review sessions.

4. Feedback Loop for Improvement

- Providing constructive feedback from reviews to stakeholders and authors is crucial. This feedback loop facilitates continuous improvement of the product and the activities of those involved.
- Example: After a code review, the identified issues and suggestions for improvement are communicated to the development team, allowing them to enhance code quality in subsequent iterations.

5. Adequate Review Preparation Time

- Participants should be given sufficient time to prepare for the review. Rushed reviews can lead to suboptimal outcomes.
- Example: In a technical review, reviewers should have ample time to examine the test scripts and formulate constructive comments thoroughly.

6. Management Support

- Management's backing and commitment to the review process are fundamental. It ensures that resources and time are allocated appropriately.
- Example: Management may allocate dedicated time slots for reviews in the project schedule and provide access to necessary tools and resources.

7. Integration into Organizational Culture

- Reviews should be integrated into the organisation's culture, fostering a learning and process improvement mindset.
- Example: An organisation might encourage knowledge sharing and collaborative learning through regular review sessions, making it a cultural norm.

8. **Comprehensive Training**

   - Providing adequate training to all review participants ensures they understand their roles and responsibilities in the review process.
   - Example: New team members may receive training on the organisation's review procedures and tools to ensure they contribute effectively to reviews.

9. **Effective Meeting Facilitation**

   - Facilitating review meetings efficiently and inclusively is critical to best use participants' time and expertise.
   - Example: A well-facilitated code review meeting ensures all participants can voice their opinions, leading to a more comprehensive code evaluation.

10. **Objective and Trust-Based Environment**

    - Encouraging trust where defects are welcomed and expressed objectively is essential for constructive reviews.
    - Example: Review participants should focus on the issues in the work product rather than assigning blame, fostering a collaborative and solution-oriented environment.

11. **Positive Author Experience**

    - Ensuring the author has a positive experience throughout the review process promotes a collaborative culture.
    - Example: Providing clear guidelines and support to authors can help them understand and embrace the feedback provided during the review.

In summary, the success of software reviews hinges on a combination of well-defined processes, supportive organisational culture, effective communication, and the application of these key success factors. When these elements are in place, reviews become valuable tools for enhancing product quality and team performance.

Summary

Static Testing is a crucial part of software development that involves inspecting work products without executing code. There are two primary methods:

1. **Reviews (Manual):** Involves manual examination of work products, like code and documentation, focusing on quality, correctness, and consistency. Collaboration between testers, business representatives, and developers is essential.

2. **Static Analysis (Using Tools):** Employs tools to identify issues in code and other work products, offering advantages like early issue detection and integration into Continuous Integration (CI) frameworks.

Static testing can be applied to various work products, such as specifications, code, and user documentation. Its benefits include early defect detection, low effort, and seamless integration with CI.

Differences from dynamic testing: Static testing is non-execution-based and identifies defects early, while dynamic testing involves executing code to find failures during runtime.

Advantages of early stakeholder feedback include identifying quality issues promptly, preventing misunderstandings, and enhancing communication.

The **review process** involves planning, initiation, individual review, communication, fixing, and reporting.

Roles in review processes include managers, moderators, review leaders, reviewers, authors, and scribes.

Types of reviews range from informal to formal, with varying levels of rigour. The choice depends on project requirements, complexity, and regulatory needs.

Success factors for reviews include clear objectives, appropriate review types, small-chunked reviews, feedback loops, preparation time, management support, cultural integration, comprehensive training, effective meetings, a positive environment, and a learning experience for the author. These factors contribute to the effectiveness of software reviews.

Quiz 3

1. The moderator leads a walkthrough. (True/False)
2. Entry and exit criteria are not required for inspection. (True/False)
3. The main benefit of static testing over dynamic testing is that it enables early testing. (True/False)
4. It is easier to find undefined variables by dynamic testing rather than static testing. (True/False)
5. A mature development process is a prerequisite for dynamic testing. (True/False)
6. A scribe is a person responsible for conducting inspections. (True/False)
7. The effort involved in planning for a review is not included in the review cost. (True/False)
8. The purpose of static testing is to find the defects, and that of dynamic testing is to fix them. (True/False)
9. The purpose of the inspection is to learn, gain understanding, and find defects. (True/False)

Quiz 3: Answers

1. **The moderator leads a walkthrough. (False)**

   - Justification: In a typical walkthrough, the document's author or code under review leads the session, not the moderator. The moderator's role is more prominent in inspections.

2. **Entry and exit criteria are not required for inspection. (False)**

   - Justification: Inspections are formal review processes requiring clear entry and exit criteria to ensure the inspection is conducted systematically and thoroughly.

3. **The main benefit of static testing over dynamic testing is that it enables early testing. (True)**

   - Justification: Static testing, which involves reviewing code without executing it, allows for early detection of defects, making it less costly in defect fixing than dynamic testing, which requires code execution.

4. **It is easier to find undefined variables by dynamic testing rather than static testing. (False)**

   - Justification: Undefined variables are typically identified during static testing, such as through compiler checks, rather than during dynamic testing, which involves running the code.

5. **A mature development process is a prerequisite for dynamic testing. (True)**

   - Justification: A mature development process ensures that all necessary conditions, like test environment availability, are in place for effective dynamic testing, where the code is executed and tested under various conditions.

6. **A scribe is a person responsible for conducting inspections. (False)**

   - Justification: In inspections, the trained moderators, not scribes, lead the process. The scribe's role is typically to record findings and decisions, not to conduct the inspection.

7. **The effort involved in planning for a review is not included in the review cost. (False)**

   - Justification: Planning for a review is a significant activity that requires effort and resources; therefore, it should be included in the overall cost of the review process.

8. **The purpose of static testing is to find the defects, and that of dynamic testing is to fix them. (False)**

   - Justification: The primary purpose of static and dynamic testing is to find defects in the software. Fixing these defects is a separate process following the testing phase.

9. **The purpose of the inspection is to learn, gain understanding, and find defects. (False)**

   - Justification: The primary purpose of a walkthrough is for learning, gaining understanding, and defect-finding. On the other hand, inspections are more formal and primarily focused on defect identification.

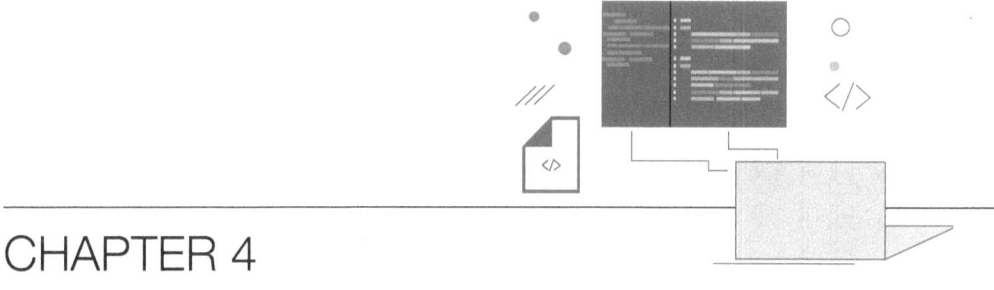

CHAPTER 4

TEST ANALYSIS AND DESIGN

(11 QUESTIONS | 390 MINUTES)

Learning Objectives for Chapter 4

4.1 Test Techniques Overview

- FL-4.1.1 (K2) Distinguish black-box, white-box and experience-based test techniques

4.2 Black-box Test Techniques

- FL-4.2.1 (K3) Use equivalence partitioning to derive test cases
- FL-4.2.2 (K3) Use boundary value analysis to derive test cases
- FL-4.2.3 (K3) Use decision table testing to derive test cases
- FL-4.2.4 (K3) Use state transition testing to derive test cases

4.3 White-box Test Techniques

- FL-4.3.1 (K2) Explain statement testing
- FL-4.3.2 (K2) Explain branch testing
- FL-4.3.3 (K2) Explain the value of white-box testing

4.4 Experience-based Test Techniques

- FL-4.4.1 (K2) Explain error guessing
- FL-4.4.2 (K2) Explain exploratory testing
- FL-4.4.3 (K2) Explain checklist-based testing

4.5. Collaboration-based Test Approaches

- FL-4.5.1 (K2) Explain how to write user stories in collaboration with developers and business representatives
- FL-4.5.2 (K2) Classify the different options for writing acceptance criteria
- FL-4.5.3 (K3) Use acceptance test-driven development (ATDD) to derive test cases

4.1 Test Techniques Overview

Understanding the various test techniques is essential for testers to determine what and how to test effectively. These techniques aid in the development of a manageable set of test cases and help testers define test conditions and identify suitable test data. Let's explore the world of test techniques and their classifications and significance.

The Role of Test Techniques:

Test techniques serve two primary purposes:

1. **Test Analysis:** These techniques guide testers in determining what aspects of the software to test. They help define test conditions and identify coverage items.

2. **Test Design:** They provide insights into how to test by helping testers create test cases and identify the necessary test data. Test techniques enable testers to reduce the number of test cases to a manageable level while maintaining test effectiveness.

Factors Influencing Test Technique Selection:

The choice of test technique is influenced by various factors, including:

- Component or system complexity
- Regulatory standards
- Customer or contractual requirements
- Risk levels and types
- Availability of documentation
- Tester knowledge and skills
- Available tools
- Time and budget constraints
- Software Development Lifecycle Model (SDLC)
- Types of defects expected in the component or system

Example Scenarios:

- **Exploratory Testing:** When minimal or no documentation is available, exploratory testing becomes valuable. Testers rely on their intuition and skills to uncover issues.
- **Agile Deployment:** In Agile projects, experience-based test design techniques complement black-box and white-box techniques. Agile's iterative nature benefits from the adaptability of experience-based testing.
- **Contractual Requirements:** If a project has a contractual obligation to achieve 90% branch coverage, the team must perform testing to prove that the required coverage is met.

Categories of Test Techniques:

1. Black-box Test Techniques

- Also known as Requirement-based, Specification-based or Behaviour-Based Test Techniques
- Focus on inputs and outputs without considering the internal structure.
- Derived from software requirements, specifications, use cases, or user stories.
- Coverage is based on tested items in the test basis and the applied technique.

2. White-box Test Techniques

- Also known as Structural or Glass-box Test Techniques
- Concentrate on the internal structure and processing within the test object.
- Derived from code, software architecture, detailed design, or other structural information.
- Coverage is based on tested items within a selected structure and the applied technique.

3. **Experience-Based Test Techniques:**

- Leverage the knowledge and experience of developers, testers, and users.
- Derived from insights gained from stakeholders' experience, expected software use, environmental factors, likely defects, and their distribution.
- Often used with black-box and white-box techniques to enhance test effectiveness.

For a more in-depth exploration of test techniques and their corresponding coverage measures, refer to the ISO/IEC/IEEE 29119-4 standard.

In conclusion, mastering test techniques is fundamental for testers to navigate the complex software testing landscape. These techniques empower testers to make informed decisions about what and how to test, ultimately ensuring the delivery of high-quality software. Test techniques play a vital role in making software more effective and efficient. Effective in finding defects and efficiently utilising less time, effort, resources, and cost.

4.2 Black-box Test Techniques

4.2.1 Equivalence Partitioning (EP)

Equivalence partitioning (EP) is a valuable black box testing technique that efficiently tests various system data inputs, outputs, and parameters. This technique divides data into partitions, also known as equivalence classes, based on the expectation that all elements within a given partition will be processed similarly by the test object. Equivalence partitions can be applied to different aspects of the test object, including inputs, outputs, configuration items, internal values, time-related values, and interface parameters.

Creating Equivalence Partitions:

- **Valid Partitions:** These contain values that the system should accept and process. They align with the expected behaviour defined by the system's specification.
- **Invalid Partitions:** These encompass values that the system should reject or ignore. They may also include values for which the system's behaviour is undefined.

Characteristics of Equivalence Partitions:

- Partitions can be continuous or discrete, ordered or unordered, finite or infinite.
- Partitions must not overlap, ensuring that each value belongs to only one partition, and all partitions must be non-empty sets.

Assumption Behind Equivalence Partitioning: Equivalence partitioning operates on the premise that if a test case examining one value from an equivalence partition works fine, then any other value within the same partition should also work the same way. Consequently, testing just one value from each partition is sufficient to achieve 100% equivalence partition coverage but may not uncover potential issues.

Challenges in Applying Equivalence Partitioning: Equivalence partitioning is straightforward for simple test objects but can become intricate in practice when dealing with complex systems. Understanding how the system will treat different values often requires careful consideration.

Achieving 100% Coverage with Equivalence Partitioning: To attain complete coverage using the Equivalence Partitioning technique, test cases must exercise all identified partitions, including valid and invalid ones. Each partition should be covered by at least one test case. Coverage is quantified as the number of partitions exercised by at least one test case divided by the total number of identified partitions expressed as a percentage.

It's crucial to note that invalid partitions should be tested individually. Combining multiple invalid conditions in a single test can lead to "masking," where one failure may hide or overshadow another. For instance, if a form rejects input due to two separate validation errors but is tested with both errors in one test case, it may not be clear which error triggered the rejection. Testing invalid partitions individually ensures that each potential failure is identified and addressed separately, enhancing the thoroughness and effectiveness of the testing process.

Handling Multiple Sets of Partitions: When the test object involves multiple sets of partitions (e.g., systems with more than one input parameter), the most straightforward coverage criterion is "Each Choice" coverage. This criterion mandates that test cases must cover every partition from each set of partitions at least once. It does not consider combinations of partitions, focusing solely on individual partitions.

Application of Equivalence Partitioning: Equivalence partitioning is a versatile testing technique applicable at all levels of testing. It provides a structured approach to systematically test a system's inputs, outputs, and parameters.

Consideration of Dependencies: Testers should be mindful of potential dependencies between equivalence partitions of different parameters. For instance, in a flight reservation system, the "accompanying adult" parameter may only be relevant in combination with the age class "child." Such dependencies must be accounted for during testing to ensure comprehensive coverage.

Equivalence Partitioning is a fundamental technique in the testing arsenal. It enables efficient and effective testing by categorising inputs and values into manageable and testable partitions.

4.2.2 Boundary Value Analysis (BVA)

Boundary Value Analysis (BVA) is a valuable testing technique that extends the principles of Equivalence Partitioning (EP). It is beneficial for situations involving ordered partitions with numeric or sequential data. The fundamental concept behind BVA is to explore the behaviour of a system at its boundary values, as these are often more prone to errors than values within the partitions.

Key Aspects of Boundary Value Analysis:

1. **Identifying Boundary Values:** BVA focuses on identifying and testing the boundary values for each equivalence partition. These boundary values are critical as they are more likely to be the source of defects in the software.

2. **Applicability:** BVA can be applied at various test levels to examine requirements that involve a range of numeric values, such as dates and times.

3. **Boundary Coverage:** The effectiveness of BVA is measured in terms of boundary coverage. This metric calculates the percentage of boundary values tested compared to the total number of identified boundary test values.

Two Approaches to Boundary Value Analysis (BVA):

1. **Two-Value Approach:** In this approach, for each boundary value, there are two coverage items to test: the boundary value itself and its nearest neighbour belonging to the adjacent partition. For example, if a partition includes values from 1 to 100 in 0.5 increments, the two-value approach would test values like 0.5 and 1 for the lower boundary and 100 and 100.5 for the upper boundary.

2. **Three-Value Approach:** The three-value approach expands the testing to include all three coverage items for each boundary value: the value itself and its neighbours. Continuing the previous example, the three-value approach would examine values 0, 0.5, 1, and 1.5 for the lower boundary and 99.5, 100, 100.5, and 101 for the upper boundary.

Choosing the Approach: The two approaches depend on the perceived risk associated with the test object under test. The three-value approach is typically used for higher-risk items because it provides more comprehensive testing.

Advantages of 3-Value BVA over 2-Value BVA

3-value BVA offers a more rigorous testing approach and can uncover defects that might go unnoticed with 2-value BVA. For instance, consider the scenario where a decision in the code is implemented as "if (x ≤ 10)", but it should have been "if (x = 10)". When using the two-value BVA, tests for x = 10 and x = 11 would pass, missing the defect. However, with 3-value BVA, the test for x = 9 would fail, correctly identifying the defect and ensuring robust software quality.

In summary, Boundary Value Analysis (BVA) is a powerful testing technique that helps ensure software reliability by examining boundary values within ordered partitions. The choice between the two-value and three-value approaches should be made based on the risk associated with the specific testing scenario. Utilising 3-value BVA when appropriate enhances the thoroughness of testing and minimises the chances of defects slipping through the cracks.

Boundary Value Analysis vs Equivalence Partitioning

Equivalence Partitioning (EP) and Boundary Value Analysis (BVA) are complementary techniques to design test cases. These techniques are particularly effective in identifying defects related to input validation. To illustrate their use, consider a requirement for a field in a form that accepts whole numbers between 1 and 100, inclusive.

Equivalence Partitions:

Equivalence Partitioning involves dividing input data into partitions of equivalent data from which test cases can be derived. In this example, there are three partitions:

- P1: Less than 1 (Invalid)
- P2: 1 to 100 (Valid)
- P3: Greater than 100 (Invalid)

For 100% EP coverage, one test case from each partition is sufficient:

- TC1: -5 (P1)
- TC2: 40 (P2)
- TC3: 105 (P3)

Boundary Value Analysis:

Boundary Value Analysis is a technique that focuses on the values at the boundaries of equivalence partitions. It is based on the observation that errors occur at the edges of input ranges. For this example, the boundaries are 1 and 100. Hence, the test cases include:

- TC1: 0 (P1)
- TC2: 1 (P2)

- TC3: 100 (P2)
- TC4: 101 (P3)

100% BVA coverage ensures 100% EP coverage but not vice versa. This principle is evident when examining the code logic for the requirement, which ideally should be:

> IF (0 < X < 101):
>   'Do something VALID'
> ELSE:
>   'Do something INVALID'

However, if the developer makes a mistake and uses ten instead of 0 in the lower bound:

> IF (10 < X < 101):
>   'Do something VALID'
> ELSE:
>   'Do something INVALID'

In such a scenario, BVA proves more effective as it can identify the failure when the boundary value of 1 is tested (TC2: 1 (P2) - FAIL), while EP might miss this since all its test cases would pass. The increased effectiveness of BVA comes at the cost of more test cases, which implies additional time, effort, and cost.

In summary:

EP Test Cases:
- TC1: -5 (P1) - PASS
- TC2: 40 (P2) - PASS
- TC3: 105 (P3) - PASS

BVA Test Cases:
- TC1: 0 (P1) - PASS
- TC2: 1 (P2) - FAIL
- TC3: 100 (P2) - PASS
- TC4: 101 (P3) - PASS

Therefore, **BVA is generally more effective than EP** in identifying boundary-related errors in input validation.

4.2.3 Decision Table Testing

Decision table testing is a potent technique for scrutinising the implementation of system requirements, mainly when dealing with intricate scenarios where different combinations of conditions (inputs) yield distinct outcomes (decisions, actions). This method is invaluable when handling complex logic, such as business rules.

Creating Decision Tables:

- Decision tables define the system's conditions (inputs) and the resulting actions (outputs or decisions).
- Rows within the table depict diverse combinations of conditions, while each column corresponds to a unique decision rule, associating conditions with actions.
- Conditions and actions are typically represented using Boolean values (true or false), though other data types, such as ranges or discrete values, can also be incorporated.
- The notational conventions employed include "T" for true, "F" for false, "-" for irrelevant conditions, and "N/A" for infeasible conditions. Actions are indicated by "X" for occurrence and a blank space for non-occurrence.

Example - ATM Cash Withdrawal:

- To illustrate, consider a scenario where a customer requests a cash withdrawal from an ATM.
- The business rules governing the ATM are twofold:

1. The ATM disburses the amount if the customer has sufficient funds.
2. The ATM dispenses the amount if the customer has been granted credit.

The Full Decision Table for the above requirement is shown below:

Conditions	R1	R2	R3	R4
C1: Withdrawal Amount <= Balance	T	T	F	F
C2: Credit Granted	T	F	T	F
Actions				
A1: Withdrawal Granted	T	T	T	F

Full Decision Table

Here, with this decision table, there is an opportunity to collapse R1 and R2 together. This is feasible as the second condition, "Credit granted", does not affect the outcome.

A collapsed decision table where R1 and R2 are collapsed into a single rule is as below:

Conditions	R1	R3	R4
C1: Withdrawal Amount <= Balance	T	F	F
C2: Credit Granted	-	T	F
Actions			
A1: Withdrawal Granted	T	T	F

Collapsed Decision Table

Here, "-" denotes that the condition doesn't matter (don't care).

Simplifying Decision Tables:

- Decision tables can become intricate, but their complexity can be reduced by removing columns containing infeasible conditions combinations.
- Columns of housing conditions that do not impact the outcome can be merged into a single column.
- In-depth minimisation algorithms for decision tables are beyond the scope of this discussion.

Coverage in Decision Table Testing:

- In the domain of decision table testing, the primary objective is to test the columns that represent viable combinations of conditions.
- Achieving comprehensive coverage entails testing all these columns.
- Coverage is quantified by the ratio of exercised columns (rules) to the total number of feasible columns (rules), expressed as a percentage.

Benefits of Decision Table Testing:

- Decision table testing offers a structured approach for recognising all potential condition combinations, ensuring none are overlooked.
- It is instrumental in uncovering gaps or contradictions in requirements.
- However, when grappling with numerous conditions, testing all decision rules can be time-consuming, owing to the exponential proliferation of rules with increasing conditions.
- In such scenarios, adopting a minimised decision table or a risk-based approach can alleviate the burden by reducing the number of rules requiring testing.

Types of Decision Tables:

- Decision tables can be classified into two principal categories: limited entry and extended entry.

In summary, decision table testing represents an asset for systematically assessing software behaviour across various permutations of conditions. It proves instrumental in detecting issues, validating requirements, and optimising testing endeavours, cementing its status as an indispensable technique in the software testing arsenal.

4.2.4 State Transition Testing

State Transition Testing is a valuable technique for assessing a system's behaviour by modelling its various states and valid transitions between them. This method benefits applications with discrete states and well-defined transitions, such as menu-based software, embedded systems, or screen navigation scenarios.

Understanding State Transition Diagrams

A state transition diagram provides a visual representation of the system's behaviour. It displays:

- **Possible software states** represent the various conditions or modes the software can be in.
- **Transitions between states:** These indicate how the software moves from one state to another.
- **Events:** Events initiate transitions, which guard conditions can further qualify.
- **Actions:** Transitions may trigger actions or operations in the software.

Typically, transitions in a state transition diagram are labelled with the syntax: "event [guard condition] / action." If guard conditions or actions are not relevant, they can be omitted. These transitions are assumed to be instantaneous and can lead to software actions.

The Role of State Tables

A state table serves as an equivalent model to a state transition diagram. It presents the same information but in a tabular format. In a state table:

- Rows represent states.
- Columns represent events (including guard conditions, if any).
- Table entries (cells) represent transitions, indicating the target state and associated actions if defined.

One notable advantage of state tables is that they explicitly show invalid transitions by having empty cells, which can benefit testing.

Creating Test Cases

Test cases based on state transition diagrams or tables are usually expressed as sequences of events. These event sequences lead to state changes and, when necessary, trigger actions. A single test case often covers multiple transitions between states.

Coverage Criteria in State Transition Testing

State transition testing employs various coverage criteria to ensure thorough testing. This book discusses three primary criteria:

1. All States Coverage:

- Coverage Item: States
- Objective: Ensure that test cases visit all states.
- Measurement: Calculate the percentage of visited states out of the total states.

2. Valid Transitions Coverage (0-Switch Coverage):

- Coverage Item: Single valid transitions
- Objective: Exercise all valid transitions.

- Measurement: Determine the percentage of exercised valid transitions out of the total valid transitions.
- Note: Achieving full valid transitions coverage inherently guarantees all states coverage.

3. All Transitions Coverage:

- Coverage Item: All transitions shown in a state table (both valid and invalid)
- Objective: Exercise all valid transitions and attempt to execute invalid ones.
- Measurement: Calculate the percentage of valid and attempted invalid transitions covered by executed test cases out of the total valid and invalid transitions.
- Importance: Essential for mission and safety-critical software as it ensures full coverage of all states and valid transitions, thus avoiding fault masking.

State Transition Testing is valuable for assessing software behaviour in discrete state-based systems. Understanding state transition diagrams, tables, and coverage criteria is crucial for designing effective test cases and ensuring comprehensive testing, especially in critical software applications.

Example 1:

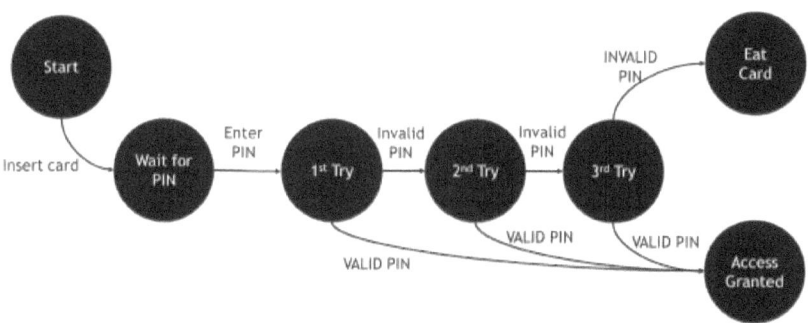

State Transition Diagram for ATM Machine

For the above-state transition diagram for the ATM Machine, we need 4 test cases to have 100% valid state transition coverage in this example.

- TC1: Start -> Wait for PIN -> 1st Try -> 2nd Try -> 3rd Try -> Eat Card
- TC2: Start -> Wait for PIN -> 1st Try -> 2nd Try -> 3rd Try -> Access Granted
- TC3: Start -> Wait for PIN -> 1st Try -> 2nd Try -> Access Granted
- TC4: Start -> Wait for PIN -> 1st Try -> Access Granted

Example 2:

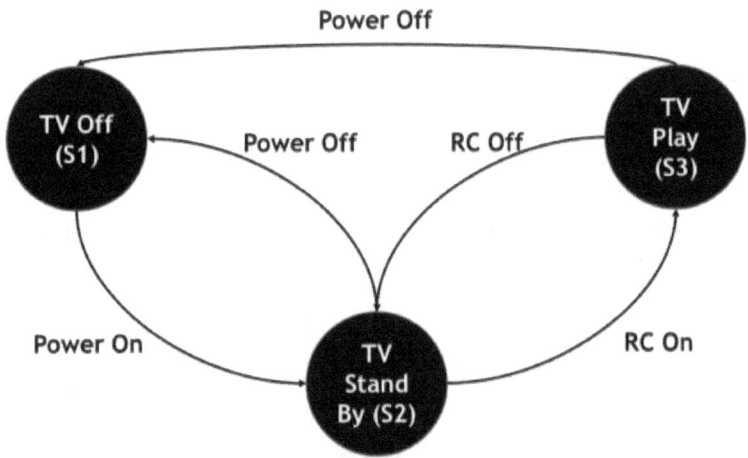

State Transition Diagram for TV

In this description, we are considering a system that can exist in one of three states (S1, S2, S3) and respond to four different actions (Power On, Power Off, RC On, RC Off). The task is to understand and define the transitions between these states based on the given actions.

1. **Total Possible Transitions:**

   With three states and four actions, the total theoretical number of state-action combinations is 12. This is calculated by multiplying the number of states (3) by the number of actions (4). These combinations represent all the potential transitions without considering whether they are valid or not in the context of the system.

2. **Valid Transitions:**

   Out of these 12 potential transitions, only five are identified as valid. Valid transitions are meaningful and allowed within the system's logic. These are represented by arrows in a state transition diagram, indicating the flow from one state to another under specific actions.

3. **Invalid Transitions:**

   The number of invalid transitions is determined by subtracting the number of valid transitions from the total possible transitions. In this case, 12 (total) - 5 (valid) = seven invalid transitions. These transitions are not permitted or do not result in a state change within the system, either because they are logically inconsistent or because the system does not support such changes under the given conditions.

4. **Decision Table for Invalid Transitions:**

   A decision table is used to understand these seven invalid transitions. A decision table is a tabular representation that helps understand how different input combinations (in this case, states and actions) will lead to different outcomes (transitions). The table will show whether the transition is valid for each state-action pair. This is particularly useful for identifying the invalid transitions, as it delineates which combinations of state and action do not result in a meaningful transition in the system.

Initial State / Condition	Power On	Power Off	RC On	RC Off
S1: TV Off	S2	-	-	-
S2: TV Stand By	-	S1	S3	-
S3: TV Play	-	S1	-	S2

State Table

By creating such a decision table, one can easily map out the logic of the system's transitions and identify which transitions are allowed and which are not, aiding in understanding and testing the system effectively.

4.3 White-box Test Techniques

White-box testing techniques are an essential part of software quality assurance. They provide a deep insight into a software application's inner workings, helping identify and eliminate defects early in development. In this chapter, we will explore two popular white-box test techniques: Statement testing and Branch testing.

4.3.1 Statement Testing and Coverage

Statement testing is a white-box technique that tests executable statements within the code. The primary objective of statement testing is to ensure that all executable statements in the code are tested thoroughly. Let's delve into the details:

What is Statement Testing? Statement testing involves designing test cases that exercise individual statements in the code. The goal is to achieve maximum code coverage, meaning every executable statement is executed at least once.

Coverage Measurement: Coverage is measured as a percentage, calculated by dividing the number of executed statements by the total number of executable statements in the code. For example, if 100 executable statements and test cases exercise 80, the statement coverage would be 80%.

Advantages of Statement Testing:

- Helps identify potential errors or bugs in the code.
- Provides an objective measurement of code coverage.
- Aims for thorough testing of the code's logic.

Limitations: Statement testing has its limitations. It may not detect data-dependent defects, such as a division by zero that only fails when a specific condition is met. Additionally, achieving 100% statement coverage does not guarantee that all decision logic has been tested, as it may not cover all branches in the code.

Example 1: Let's consider a simple code snippet with if-endif:

```
if x > 0:
        result = x * 2
endif
```

To achieve 100% statement coverage, we need only one test case that exercises the if-endif statement's "result = x*2" statement.

Example 2: Let's consider a simple code snippet with if-else-endif:

```
if x > 0:
        result = x * 2
Else:
        result = x + 1
endif
```

To achieve 100% statement coverage, we need two test cases that exercise both branches of the if-else statement.

4.3.2 Branch Testing and Coverage

Branch testing is another crucial white box technique that tests control flow branches within the code. Let's explore branch testing in detail:

What is Branch Testing? Branch testing involves designing test cases to exercise branches in the code. A branch represents a transfer of control between two nodes in the control flow graph. These branches can be unconditional (straight-line code) or conditional (resulting from decisions).

Coverage Measurement: Branch coverage is measured as a percentage, calculated by dividing the number of exercised branches by the total number of branches in the code. Achieving 100% branch coverage means that all unconditional and conditional branches have been tested.

Advantages of Branch Testing:

- Ensures thorough testing of control flow and decision-making in the code.
- Provides an objective measurement of code coverage.
- Helps identify defects related to branching logic.

Limitations: Branch testing, like statement testing, has limitations. It may not detect defects requiring the execution of specific paths in the code.

Example 1: Let's consider a simple code snippet with if-endif:

> *If temperature > 30:*
>   *activateCoolingSystem()*
> *Endif*

To achieve 100% branch coverage, we need two test cases that cover both branches (activating the cooling system and not activating the cooling system) of the if-endif statement.

Example 2: Consider a code snippet with a decision branch:

> *If temperature > 30:*
>   *activateCoolingSystem()*
> *Else:*
>   *notifyUser("Temperature is normal")*
> *endif*

To achieve 100% branch coverage, we need two test cases that cover both branches (activate the cooling system and display the message "Temperature is normal") of the if-else statement.

4.3.3 The Value of White-box Testing

White-box testing techniques offer several advantages:

- They consider the entire software implementation, making them suitable for detecting defects even when the software specification is vague, outdated, or incomplete.
- White-box techniques can be used in static testing, which means they are valuable for reviewing code before execution, including pseudocode and high-level logic.
- They provide objective code coverage measurements, enabling teams to generate additional tests to increase coverage and boost confidence in the code's quality.

However, it's important to note that white-box testing may still miss defects related to unimplemented requirements.

In conclusion, white box testing techniques like statement and branch testing are powerful tools for ensuring software quality. They provide a deep understanding of code behaviour and help uncover defects early in development. By measuring code coverage objectively, teams can enhance their testing efforts and build more robust software systems.

4.4 Experience-based Test Techniques

Experience-based test techniques are valuable tools that draw upon the expertise and knowledge of testers. They do not rely on formal specifications but rather on the insights and intuition of the testing team. This section will explore three commonly used experience-based test techniques: Error Guessing, Exploratory Testing, and Checklist-Based Testing.

4.4.1 Error Guessing

Error guessing is a technique that allows testers to anticipate the occurrence of errors, defects, and failures based on their accumulated knowledge and experience. Testers draw upon several key sources of information:

- **Past Application Behaviour:** Understanding how the application has performed historically can provide valuable insights into where errors may lurk.
- **Developer Error Patterns:** Recognizing common mistakes made by developers and the resulting defects can help testers pinpoint potential issues.
- **Similar Application Failures:** Examining failures in similar applications can shed light on vulnerabilities in the software under test.

Errors, defects, and failures can manifest in various ways, such as incorrect inputs, flawed logic, computation errors, interface mismatches, or data issues. A systematic approach to error guessing involves creating a list of possible errors, defects, and failures based on these sources of knowledge. Test cases are then designed to uncover or expose these issues.

For example, if historical data suggests that users often encounter problems with incorrect input formats, a test case could be devised to deliberately input data incorrectly to see how the application responds.

4.4.2 Exploratory Testing

Exploratory testing takes a different approach by allowing testers to simultaneously design, execute, and evaluate tests while actively learning about the test object. It is precious when formal specifications are lacking or time constraints are pressing.

Testers delve into the application during exploratory testing to gain a deeper understanding. They may start with broad, high-level tests and gradually refine their approach as they uncover aspects of the software that warrant further scrutiny. Testers document their findings, including defects, thoughts on further testing, and what has been tested.

One structured approach to exploratory testing is session-based testing. In this method, exploratory testing occurs within a defined time frame, guided by a test charter that outlines test objectives. The session concludes with a debriefing session involving stakeholders interested in the test results.

Exploratory testing shines when there is a lack of comprehensive specifications or when time pressures necessitate agile testing approaches. It can also complement more formal test techniques, allowing testers to uncover unexpected issues that might go unnoticed.

Example Test Charter:

Title: User Login Functionality (90 mins test session)

Actor: Test Engineer: Alex Johnson

Purpose: To validate the functionality, security, and user experience of the user login process in the "MyApp" application.

Setup:

- **Environment:** Test server with the latest version of "MyApp" installed.

- **Tools:** Browser (Chrome, Firefox, Safari), Database access tools, and Network monitoring software.
- **Access:** Test accounts with various permission levels.

Priority: High (critical for application security and user access)

References:

- **Design Specifications:** Document ID 12345 - "User Login Requirements"
- **Security Protocols:** Document ID 67890 - "Application Security Guidelines"

Data:

- Usernames and passwords for test accounts (normal user, admin, locked accounts)
- Usernames and passwords for boundary testing (invalid, expired, special characters)

List of Activities:

- **Verify Login with Valid and Invalid Credentials:** Test login functionality using valid and invalid user credentials.
- **Assess Security Against SQL Injection:** Conduct SQL injection tests to ensure login security.
- **Evaluate Secure Credential Transmission:** Check for HTTPS usage during login credential transmission.
- **Measure Login Response Time:** Analyse the response time during the login process for user experience.
- **Review Clarity of Error Messages**: Assess the clarity and appropriateness of error messages on failed login attempts.
- **Browser Compatibility Testing:** Test login functionality across different web browsers.

- **Test Account Lockout Mechanism:** Verify the account lockout process after multiple failed login attempts.
- **Validate Password Reset Process:** Test the entire password reset process, including link expiration.
- **Check Session Management Post-Login and Logout:** Ensure proper session management, including termination post-logout.
- **Two-Factor Authentication Functionality Check:** Test and validate the two-factor authentication process if applicable.

4.4.3 Checklist-Based Testing

Checklist-based testing involves designing, implementing, and executing tests based on a predefined checklist of test conditions. These checklists are created based on the tester's experience, understanding of user requirements, and knowing why and how software can fail.

Each item in the checklist is typically phrased as a question, making verifying it straightforward. The checklist covers various aspects, including requirements, graphical interface properties, quality characteristics, and other test conditions.

Checklists are dynamic documents that evolve. As testers gain experience and identify new defects, they can update the checklist to reflect these findings. However, it's crucial to strike a balance and avoid making the checklist overly lengthy.

In cases where detailed test cases are lacking, checklist-based testing provides guidelines and consistency for the testing process. While it may introduce some variability due to its high-level nature, it offers the potential for more excellent test coverage and valuable insights into software quality.

Example:

Pre-Flight Checklist for Ground Staff: Aircraft Safety and Readiness

1. **Exterior Inspection**

   - Check for any visible damage to the aircraft body (dents, cracks, corrosion).
   - Ensure all doors, hatches, and cargo holds are locked securely.
   - Verify that tires are correctly inflated and show no wear or damage.
   - Inspect the wings and tail for structural integrity.

2. **Engine and Fuel System**

   - Confirm that engine cowls are secured and show no signs of leaks.
   - Check fuel levels and ensure there are no signs of fuel leakage.
   - Verify the proper functioning of fuel caps and seals.

3. **Landing Gear**

   - Inspect the landing gear for any signs of damage or hydraulic leaks.
   - Ensure that the landing gear doors are properly closed.

4. **Flight Control Surfaces**

   - Verify that ailerons, elevators, and rudders are secure and have full range of motion.
   - Check for any obstructions or foreign objects that could impede movement.

5. **Cockpit and Cabin**

   - Ensure that cockpit instruments and controls are functioning correctly.
   - Check that all cabin emergency exits are operational and marked.
   - Verify that seat belts are functioning and in good condition.

- Confirm the availability and proper placement of safety equipment (life vests, oxygen masks).

6. **Lighting and Electrical Systems**

   - Test navigation and communication systems for functionality.
   - Check all external and internal lights (landing lights, cabin lights) for operation.

7. **Environmental and Weather Check**

   - Review current and forecasted weather conditions.
   - Ensure that deicing has been performed if necessary.

8. **Documentation and Compliance**

   - Verify that all necessary flight documents (flight plans, manuals, logbooks) are on board.
   - Confirm compliance with any specific regulatory requirements for the flight.

9. **Communication with the Flight Crew**

   - Brief the flight crew on the status of the aircraft and any issues noted during the inspection.
   - Confirm that the flight crew has completed their pre-flight checks and is ready for departure.

10. **Final Clearance**

    - Ensure all ground support equipment is removed and clear of the aircraft.
    - Conduct a final walk-around inspection.
    - Provide clearance to the flight crew for engine start and taxi.

Note: This checklist is a general guide and may need to be adapted to specific aircraft models and airline procedures. Safety and compliance with aviation regulations should always be the top priority.

In summary, experience-based test techniques, such as Error Guessing, Exploratory Testing, and Checklist-Based Testing, offer flexible and effective approaches to uncovering defects and improving software quality. These techniques leverage testers' collective knowledge and expertise, making them valuable additions to a tester's toolbox.

4.5 Collaboration-based Test Approaches

In software testing, we have various techniques at our disposal to detect defects in our applications. We've explored Black-box, White-box, and Experience-based testing techniques in previous sections. These techniques are primarily geared towards identifying defects in the software. However, another testing dimension focuses on defect detection and avoidance through improved collaboration and communication among team members. This is where collaboration-based test approaches come into play.

Collaboration-based test approaches go beyond merely finding and fixing defects. They emphasise working together to prevent defects from arising in the first place. Let's delve into some key aspects of collaboration-based testing.

4.5.1 Collaborative User Story Writing

In Agile software development, user stories are fundamental building blocks. They represent features or functionality that will bring value to users or customers. Collaborative user story writing involves gathering input and insights from team members, including developers, testers, and business representatives.

Why Collaborative User Stories?

User stories are essential in Agile, but poorly defined ones can lead to project failures. Common issues include a lack of understanding of actual needs, a lack of a global vision for the system, redundant or contradictory features, and miscommunications.

Collaborative techniques like brainstorming and mind mapping help capture user story requirements and acceptance criteria involving different perspectives. This collaboration ensures everyone is on the same page, reducing misunderstandings and improving the quality of user stories.

User Story Format

In Agile software development, the User Story format is a concise and user-centred way to express requirements. A User Story typically follows a structured format that includes:

1. **Role (Who needs?):** This represents the persona or the user role for the feature being developed. It clarifies who will benefit from the functionality.

2. **Goal (What is needed? Feature/function):** The goal describes what the user intends to achieve or what problem they need to solve using the software. It provides context for the development team.

3. **Benefit (Why is it needed? The value):** This part outlines the value or benefit the user or the business will gain from the feature. It helps the team understand the significance of the functionality.

4. **Acceptance Criteria:** Acceptance criteria are the specific conditions or criteria that must be met for the User Story to be considered complete and accepted by stakeholders. They define the boundaries of the story and the expected behaviour.

Example User Story:

"As a **registered user** (Role), I want to **reset my password** (Goal) so that I can **regain access to my account** (Benefit)."

Acceptance Criteria:

- When I click the 'Forgot Password' link, I should receive an email with a password reset link.
- The password reset link should expire after 24 hours.
- After clicking the reset link, I should be able to create a new password and regain access to my account.

User Story Creation Techniques

Two standard techniques for collaborative user story creation are:

- **Brainstorming** encourages team members to generate as many ideas as possible without criticism. Wild and ambitious ideas are welcomed, and participants are encouraged to build on each other's ideas.
- **Mind Mapping:** This powerful visual technique effectively helps organise ideas and information.

Remember the acronym INVEST, which stands for Independent, Negotiable, Valuable, Estimable, Small, and Testable. Good user stories should exhibit these qualities.

INVEST Principle for User Stories

The INVEST principle is a set of characteristics that define well-formed User Stories. It helps ensure that User Stories are valuable and practical. INVEST stands for:

1. **Independent:** User Stories should be independent of each other, meaning they can be developed and tested in any order without dependencies on other stories.

2. **Negotiable:** User Stories should be open to negotiation and discussion. They should not be overly detailed or rigid, allowing room for collaboration and changes.

3. **Valuable:** Each User Story should deliver value to the end user or the business. It should focus on solving real problems or providing meaningful benefits.

4. **Estimable:** The development team should be able to estimate the size or effort required to complete the User Story. If it's too vague or complex, estimation becomes challenging.

5. **Small:** User Stories should be small enough to be completed within a single iteration or sprint. Smaller stories are easier to manage and deliver more quickly.

6. **Testable:** User Stories should have clear and measurable Acceptance Criteria. They should be testable to ensure that they meet the desired outcome.

3-C Concept for User Stories

The 3-C concept is a fundamental aspect of writing compelling User Stories. It stands for:

1. **Card:** The "Card" represents the physical or digital card where the User Story is documented. It's a concise and portable format, often found on a physical card or a digital board.

2. **Conversation:** The "Conversation" aspect emphasises that the details of the User Story should be discussed and elaborated through conversations within the development team. It's not just about writing requirements; it's about engaging in discussions to ensure a shared understanding.

3. **Confirmation:** "Confirmation" refers to the Acceptance Criteria associated with the User Story. These criteria define the specific conditions that must be met for the User Story to be considered done and ready for acceptance by stakeholders. They serve as a checklist for completeness.

By adhering to the User Story format, the 3-C concept, and the INVEST principle, Agile teams can create well-defined, user-focused stories that facilitate effective communication, collaboration, and the delivery of valuable software features.

4.5.2 Acceptance Criteria

Acceptance criteria are essential for defining the scope of a user story and achieving stakeholder consensus. They help describe positive and negative scenarios and serve as the basis for user story acceptance testing. Properly defined acceptance criteria also facilitate accurate planning and estimation.

Common Formats for Acceptance Criteria

Acceptance criteria can take different formats, but two common ones are:

- **Scenario-Oriented:** This format follows the Given/When/Then structure often used in Behaviour-Driven Development (BDD).
- **Rule-Oriented:** This format can include a bullet-point verification list or tabulated input-output mapping.
- **Custom formats** are allowed if they are clear, well-defined, and unambiguous.

Acceptance criteria should address various topics, including functional behaviour, quality characteristics, scenarios (use cases), business rules, external interfaces, constraints, and data definitions.

4.5.3 Acceptance Test-Driven Development (ATDD)

Acceptance Test-Driven Development (ATDD) is a collaborative, test-first approach in software development. It focuses on defining and creating test cases before implementing user stories. This methodology involves stakeholders, including business customers, developers, and testers, to ensure a comprehensive understanding and coverage of the requirements.

The ATDD process typically involves:

- **A specification workshop** where the user story and acceptance criteria are analysed, discussed, and written collectively.

- **Creating test cases** based on the acceptance criteria, often using natural language to describe preconditions, inputs, and postconditions.
- **Ensuring comprehensive coverage** of all user story characteristics within its scope.

Benefits of ATDD:

- Enhances communication and collaboration among team members.
- Leads to a deeper and shared understanding of the user requirements.
- Promotes early detection and resolution of defects.
- Creates a repository of reusable tests for regression testing.
- Ensures that the software meets the business needs and quality standards.

ATDD promotes not only positive testing (confirming correct behaviour) but also negative testing (identifying exceptions or error conditions) and non-functional testing (evaluating aspects like performance and usability).

When captured in a format supported by a test automation framework, developers can automate these test cases, making them executable requirements.

In Acceptance Test-Driven Development (ATDD), the focus should be crafting tests that align precisely with the specified acceptance criteria. This approach entails avoiding the inclusion of any elements not explicitly mentioned in these criteria, ensuring that the tests remain directly relevant and streamlined. Priority should be given to developing positive tests, which verify that the system functions as intended under normal conditions, before considering negative or edge-case scenarios.

Collaboration-based test approaches foster better communication, shared understanding, and proactive defect avoidance within Agile teams, ultimately leading to higher-quality software products.

Summary

Chapter 4: Test Analysis and Design provides a comprehensive overview of various software testing techniques and their applications. It emphasises the importance of understanding different test techniques for effective software testing, which aids in developing manageable test cases, defining test conditions, and identifying suitable test data.

The Role of Test Techniques:

1. **Test Analysis:** Guides testers in determining what to test, defining test conditions, and identifying coverage items.

2. **Test Design:** Helps create test cases and identify necessary test data, enabling testers to maintain test effectiveness while managing the number of test cases.

Factors Influencing Test Technique Selection

Selection depends on factors like component complexity, regulatory standards, customer requirements, risk levels, documentation availability, tester skills, tools, time and budget constraints, the SDLC model, and expected defect types.

Categories of Test Techniques:

1. **Black-box Test Techniques:** Focus on inputs and outputs without considering internal structure. They are derived from requirements, specifications, use cases, or user stories.

2. **White-box Test Techniques:** Concentrate on internal structure and processing. It is derived from code, architecture, design, or structural information.

3. **Experience-Based Test Techniques:** Utilize the knowledge and experience of stakeholders. It is derived from insights into expected software use, environmental factors, and likely defects.

Equivalence Partitioning Test Technique (EP): EP divides data into partitions or equivalence classes, ensuring efficient testing of various data inputs and parameters. It includes valid and invalid partitions, assuming that testing one value from a partition is sufficient to detect potential issues.

Boundary Value Analysis (BVA): BVA extends EP principles, focusing on boundary values within ordered partitions. It includes two approaches, Two-Value and Three-Value, with the latter providing more comprehensive testing.

Decision Table Testing: This technique is effective for complex scenarios with different combinations of conditions leading to distinct outcomes. It involves creating decision tables that map conditions to actions.

State Transition Testing: Used for applications with discrete states and transitions, this technique involves modelling states, transitions, events, and actions. Coverage criteria include all states coverage, valid transitions coverage, and all transitions coverage.

White-box Test Techniques: These techniques, including statement and branch testing, provide insights into the software's inner workings, identifying defects early in the development process.

Experience-Based Test Techniques: These techniques, such as Error Guessing, Exploratory Testing, and Checklist-Based Testing, rely on the expertise and intuition of the testing team.

Collaboration-Based Test Approaches emphasise defect prevention through improved collaboration and communication. They include collaborative user story writing, acceptance criteria, and Acceptance Test-Driven Development (ATDD).

In conclusion, mastering these test techniques is crucial for testers to navigate the complex landscape of software testing effectively and efficiently, ensuring the delivery of high-quality software.

Quiz 4

1. Test technique is used to optimise the testing efforts. (True/False)
2. There can be at least one test data for one valid equivalent class. (True/False)
3. White box testing is also called Glass-box testing. (True/False)
4. Knowledge of programming languages is required for black box testing. (True/False)
5. The purpose of measuring coverage is to find out the need for writing additional test cases. (True/False)
6. There can be only one test case for a rule of the decision table. (True/False)
7. Transitions are indicated by arrows in the state transition diagram. (True/False)
8. Experienced-based techniques are the most formal of all testing techniques. (True/False)
9. Exploratory testing is helpful in case of time pressure. (True/False)
10. In the INVEST guidelines, S stands for "Security". (True/False)

Quiz 4: Answers

1. **Test technique is used to optimise the testing efforts. (True)**
   - Justification: Testers can identify the maximum possible defects within a given timeframe using test design techniques. These techniques help make the testing process more efficient and effective by focusing on key areas likely to yield the most significant number of defects.

2. **There can be at least one test data for one valid equivalent class. (True)**
   - Justification: To apply the equivalence class technique, there must be at least one test data for each valid equivalent class. This ensures that each class is adequately tested and helps identify defects.

3. **White box testing is also called Glass-box testing. (True)**
   - Justification: According to the ISTQB (International Software Testing Qualifications Board) definition, white-box testing is also called glass-box testing. This terminology reflects the tester's ability to see through the 'box' or application being tested.

4. **Knowledge of programming languages is required for black box testing. (False)**
   - Justification: Programming knowledge is required for white box testing. In black box testing, the focus is on testing the software from an external perspective, without knowledge of the internal workings or code structure. Business or domain knowledge can be beneficial for black box testing.

5. **The purpose of measuring coverage is to find out the need for writing additional test cases. (True)**
   - Justification: Coverage measurement is crucial to identify testing gaps and determine whether additional testing is necessary. It

helps ensure that all parts of the application have been tested and that the testing is comprehensive.

6. **There can be only one test case for a rule of the decision table. (True)**

   - Justification: In decision table testing, each rule is typically represented by one test case. This ensures that each possible scenario or rule in the decision table is individually tested for correctness.

7. **Transitions are indicated by arrows in the state transition diagram. (True)**

   - Justification: In state transition testing, transitions between different states are indicated by arrows. These arrows help visualise how the system moves from one state to another, which is crucial for understanding and testing the system's behaviour.

8. **Experienced-based techniques are the most formal of all testing techniques. (False)**

   - Justification: Experience-based techniques are the most informal among all testing techniques. They rely heavily on the tester's skills, knowledge, and intuition rather than formal methodologies or processes.

9. **Exploratory testing is helpful in case of time pressure. (True)**

   - Justification: Exploratory testing is beneficial when there is inadequate specification or severe time pressure. It allows testers to quickly identify defects without requiring detailed test cases or extensive planning.

10. **In the INVEST guidelines, S stands for "Security". (False)**

    - Justification: In the INVEST guidelines, 'S' stands for 'Small'. INVEST is an acronym used in Agile software development to remember a set of criteria for assessing the quality of a user story: independent, negotiable, valuable, estimable, small, and testable.

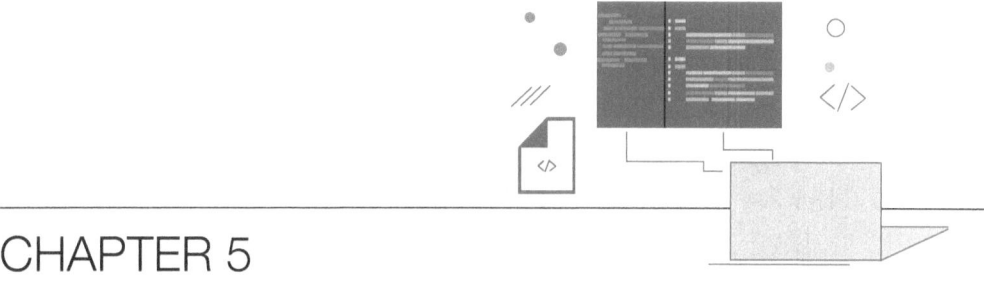

CHAPTER 5

MANAGING THE TESTING ACTIVITIES

(9 QUESTIONS | 335 MINUTES)

Learning Objectives for Chapter 5

5.1 Test Planning

- FL-5.1.1 (K2) Exemplify the purpose and content of a test plan
- FL-5.1.2 (K1) Recognize how a tester adds value to iteration and release planning
- FL-5.1.3 (K2) Compare and contrast entry criteria and exit criteria
- FL-5.1.4 (K3) Use estimation techniques to calculate the required test effort
- FL-5.1.5 (K3) Apply test case prioritization
- FL-5.1.6 (K1) Recall the concepts of the test pyramid
- FL-5.1.7 (K2) Summarize the testing quadrants and their relationships with test levels and test types

5.2 Risk Management

- FL-5.2.1 (K1) Identify risk level by using risk likelihood and risk impact
- FL-5.2.2 (K2) Distinguish between project risks and product risks

- FL-5.2.3 (K2) Explain how product risk analysis may influence thoroughness and scope of testing
- FL-5.2.4 (K2) Explain what measures can be taken in response to analysed product risks

5.3 Test Monitoring, Test Control and Test Completion

- FL-5.3.1 (K1) Recall metrics used for testing
- FL-5.3.2 (K2) Summarize the purposes, content, and audiences for test reports
- FL-5.3.3 (K2) Exemplify how to communicate the status of testing

5.4 Configuration Management

- FL-5.4.1 (K2) Summarize how configuration management supports testing

5.5 Defect Management

- FL-5.5.1 (K3) Prepare a defect report

5.1 Test Planning

Test planning is a critical phase in any software testing project. It serves as a roadmap that guides the testing process from start to finish. Here, we'll explore the purpose and content of a test plan, shedding light on its significance and components.

5.1.1 Purpose and Content of a Test Plan

Test Plan - Purpose

A test plan, at its core, is designed to achieve several key objectives:

1. **Documenting Objectives** outlines the aims, resources, and processes required for a test project.

2. **Approaches:** It defines how test objectives will be met, including means and schedules.

3. **Ensuring Compliance:** A test plan helps ensure that the test activities align with established criteria, industry standards, and legal and regulatory requirements.

4. **Communication:** It serves to communicate among team members and stakeholders.

5. **Adherence to Test Policy and Strategy:** The plan demonstrates that testing will either adhere to existing test policies and strategies or explain deviations.

Test planning compels testers to think deeply about the challenges ahead, such as risks, schedules, resource allocation, tooling, and effort required to accomplish the test project objectives.

Test Plan - Content

A well-structured test plan typically contains the following components:

1. **Context of Testing:** This section covers the scope of testing, test objectives, constraints, and the test basis. It sets the stage for what will be tested and why.

2. **Assumptions and Constraints:** It outlines any assumptions made and constraints imposed on the test project.

3. **Stakeholders:** This part identifies stakeholders, defining their roles, responsibilities, relevance to testing, and any hiring or training needs.

4. **Communication:** It addresses communication aspects, including the forms and frequency of communication and documentation templates.

5. **Risk Register:** A risk register captures product and project risks, ensuring they are accounted for and managed.

6. **Test Approach:** This critical section specifies the test levels, test types, test techniques, test deliverables, entry criteria, exit criteria, independence of testing, metrics to be collected, test data requirements, test environment requirements, and any deviations from the organisational test policy and test strategy.

7. **Budget and Schedule:** It outlines the financial and time-related aspects of the test project.

Please note that the content of test plans can vary based on project requirements and organization-specific needs. For more detailed guidance, refer to the ISO/IEC/IEEE 29119-3 standard.

Test Strategy: The test strategy describes how testing will be conducted to achieve test objectives. It is typically formulated at the product or organisational level and offers a generalised overview of the test process.

Test Approaches: Test approaches detail how the testing tasks will be implemented. They translate the test strategy into practical steps for a particular project or release. These approaches help identify test techniques, test levels, test types, entry and exit criteria, and more.

5.1.2 Planning in Agile Projects

In Agile software development, planning is a dynamic process at two key levels: release planning and iteration planning. These planning phases are essential for organising work, delivering value to the project, and ensuring alignment with project priorities.

1. Release Planning

Release planning is a high-level planning activity that focuses on delivering valuable increments of functionality. It typically spans multiple iterations and is a crucial milestone in Agile development.

Objectives:

- Define and refine the product backlog: During release planning, the product backlog is scrutinised and adjusted. Significant user stories may be broken down into smaller, more manageable ones.
- Establish the basis for the test approach and plan: Release planning lays the groundwork for testing across all iterations.
- Identify project and quality risks: Risks related to the project and product quality are identified and assessed.
- Estimate test effort: The testing effort associated with user stories is estimated.
- Plan testing activities for the release: High-level testing strategies and priorities are established for the entire release.

Testers' Role in Release Planning:

- Writing testable user stories: Testers actively participate in defining testable user stories and include acceptance criteria.

- Project and quality risk analysis: Testers contribute to identifying and assessing project and quality risks.
- Estimating test effort: Testers provide input on the effort required to test each user story.
- Determining test approaches: High-level testing strategies are outlined, aligning with the overall project goals.

2. Iteration Planning

Iteration planning is a more detailed, low-level planning activity within each iteration. It focuses on delivering specific user stories or features within a single iteration.

Objectives:

- Select user stories: The team collaboratively selects a set of user stories from the product backlog to work on during the iteration.
- Detailed risk analysis: Risk analysis is performed at a granular level, considering the specific user stories selected for the iteration.
- Testability assessment: Testers assess the testability of user stories and identify potential challenges.
- Task breakdown: User stories are divided into individual tasks, including testing tasks.
- Estimate testing effort: Testers estimate the effort required for all testing tasks associated with the user stories.
- Identify functional and non-functional aspects: Functional and non-functional testing requirements are identified and refined for the selected user stories.

Testers' Role in Iteration Planning:

- Detailed risk analysis: Testers delve deeper into risk analysis, focusing on the user stories chosen for the iteration.

- Testability assessment: Testers assess the feasibility of testing for each user story, considering its unique characteristics.
- Task breakdown: Testers participate in breaking down user stories into tasks, with a particular focus on defining testing-related tasks.
- Effort estimation: Testers estimate all testing tasks associated with the user stories.
- Functional and non-functional aspects: Testers work to identify and refine the functional and non-functional aspects of the user stories that will be tested.

In summary, release and iteration planning are fundamental activities in Agile development. Release planning sets the stage for delivering valuable increments of functionality over multiple iterations, while iteration planning focuses on the detailed work for a specific iteration. Testers play a crucial role in both planning phases by contributing their expertise in testability, risk analysis, and effort estimation, ensuring that testing aligns with the project's goals and priorities.

5.1.3 Entry Criteria and Exit Criteria

The concepts of entry and exit criteria are fundamental to ensure that the testing process is well-defined, efficient, and effective. These criteria act as gatekeepers, defining the conditions to be met before initiating or concluding a testing activity.

Entry Criteria

Entry criteria, also known as preconditions, are the set of prerequisites that must be satisfied before commencing a specific testing activity. These criteria serve as a foundation for smooth and effective testing and ensure testing can proceed without significant obstacles.

Examples of Entry Criteria:

1. **Availability of Resources:** This includes having the necessary people, tools, testing environments, test data, budget, and time to support the testing effort.

2. **Availability of Testware:** Testware, such as the test basis (requirements, user stories, specifications), testable requirements, test cases, and any other essential documentation, must be in place and accessible.

3. **Initial Quality Level of the Test Object:** Before testing begins, a basic level of quality assurance must be established. For instance, all smoke tests (basic functionality checks) may need to pass as an entry criterion.

4. **Stakeholder Alignment:** Ensure all stakeholders, including developers, testers, and relevant project members, are aligned and prepared for testing activities.

Meeting these entry criteria before initiating testing helps prevent potential roadblocks and ensures the testing effort can proceed efficiently.

Exit Criteria

Exit or completion criteria define the conditions that must be met to declare a specific testing activity or test level as completed. These criteria signal that the testing objectives have been achieved and that the testing phase can be concluded.

Examples of Exit Criteria:

1. **Measures of Thoroughness:** Exit criteria often include quantitative measures that indicate the thoroughness of testing. These may include:
   - Achieved levels of test coverage (e.g., code coverage, requirements coverage).
   - Number of unresolved defects or defect density (remaining issues).

○ Number of failed test cases (indicating issues that need resolution).

2. **Completion Criteria:** This involves ensuring that all planned tests have been executed as per the test plan, static testing (e.g., code reviews) has been performed, all identified defects have been reported, and any regression tests have been automated.

3. **Other Considerations:** Sometimes running out of time or budget can be considered valid exit criteria. If all other criteria are not satisfied, it may still be acceptable to conclude testing, provided stakeholders have reviewed and accepted the associated risks of moving forward without further testing.

In Agile Development

In Agile software development, similar criteria are applied but are often referred to as the "Definition of Done" (DoD) and "Definition of Ready" (DoR) for user stories. The Definition of Done defines the objective metrics for an item to be considered complete and potentially shippable. In contrast, the Definition of Ready outlines the preconditions a user story must fulfil before development or testing activities can commence.

In summary, entry and exit criteria play a pivotal role in the testing process by ensuring that testing activities start under favourable conditions and conclude when the predetermined testing objectives have been met. These criteria vary based on the specific testing context and are vital for maintaining the quality and effectiveness of software testing efforts.

5.1.4 Test Effort Estimations

Accurate estimation of test-related work is a pivotal aspect of project management. It involves predicting the effort required to fulfil the testing objectives of a project, release, or iteration. However, it is imperative to convey to stakeholders that estimations are inherently built on assumptions and are subject to potential errors.

Estimation Accuracy and Task Decomposition:

- Estimation accuracy typically diminishes as the scale of the task increases.
- To enhance accuracy, large tasks can be broken down into smaller, more manageable sub-tasks, each of which can be estimated individually.

1. Metrics-Based Estimation Techniques:

a. Estimation based on Ratios:

- This approach relies on historical metrics collected from previous organisational projects.
- It enables the derivation of standard ratios for projects with similar characteristics.
- For instance, if a previous project had a development-to-test effort ratio of 3:2, and the current project's development effort is estimated at 600 person-days, the test effort can be estimated at 400 person-days.

b. Extrapolation:

- This technique involves gathering measurements as early as possible in the current project.
- With sufficient data, it becomes possible to approximate the effort required for the remaining work through mathematical modelling.
- Extrapolation is well-suited for iterative Software Development Life Cycles (SDLCs). For example, a team may extrapolate test effort by averaging the effort from the last three iterations.

c. Burn-Down Charts:

- Burn-down charts are invaluable for tracking and estimating progress, especially in Agile software development.
- These charts visually represent the remaining work to be completed over time.

- As more work is accomplished, the burn-down chart shows a progress indicator moving downward, indicating the decreasing amount of estimated effort remaining in the project.
- Burn-down charts are instrumental in determining when a project or release is expected to be completed.
- They provide insights into whether the project is on track to meet its objectives based on the rate of work completed.
- In Agile development, these charts are handy for managing iterations, as they help teams assess whether they are likely to achieve their goals within the sprint.

2. Expert-Based Estimation Techniques:

a. Wideband Delphi:

- Wideband Delphi is an iterative and expert-driven technique.
- In this approach, experts independently provide estimates based on their experience.
- Deviations that fall outside predefined boundaries trigger discussions among the experts.
- Experts then re-estimate the effort, repeating the process until a consensus is reached.
- A variant of this technique known as "Planning Poker" is commonly employed in Agile software development, where estimates are represented using cards with numbers denoting the effort size.

b. Three-Point Estimation:

- Experts use this technique to provide three estimations: the most optimistic (a), the most likely (m), and the most pessimistic (b).
- The final estimate (E) is calculated as the weighted arithmetic mean: $E = (a + 4 * m + b) / 6$.
- This method also allows the experts to calculate the measurement error: $SD = (b - a) / 6$.

- For example, if estimations (in person-hours) are a=6, m=9, and b=18, the final estimation is 10±2 person-hours, signifying a range between 8 and 12 person-hours.

c. Planning Poker:

- Planning Poker is a Wideband Delphi variant often used in Agile development.
- It employs a modified Fibonacci sequence for estimation.
- The product owner presents a user story, and participants discuss assumptions and risks.
- Each participant selects a card representing their estimation, and cards are revealed simultaneously.
- High and low estimators justify their estimates, fostering discussion.
- Iterations continue until a consensus is achieved for each user story.

Factors Influencing Test Efforts

Test effort estimation is a multifaceted process considering several critical factors, each influencing the required scope and depth of testing. Understanding these factors in detail can provide a clearer picture of how they impact the estimation process.

Test effort estimation considers a variety of factors, including:

1. Product Characteristics:

- **Risks:** The higher the risk associated with a product, such as in safety-critical systems like medical devices or automotive control systems, the more extensive the testing needs.
- **Quality of the Test Basis:** A well-documented and clear test basis reduces ambiguity, leading to more efficient testing. For instance, a well-defined requirement document in a banking application can streamline the testing process.

- **Product Size and Complexity:** Larger and more complex products, like a multi-layered cloud service, require more testing effort due to the increased number of functionalities and interactions.
- **Quality Requirements:** High-quality standards, such as those in aerospace software, demand rigorous testing protocols.
- **Documentation:** Comprehensive and clear documentation can facilitate easier test case creation and execution.
- **Legal/Regulatory Compliance:** Products needing to meet specific standards, like GDPR for data protection, require additional testing to ensure compliance.

2. **Development Process:**

- **Organization Stability/Maturity**: A mature organisation with stable processes usually has a more streamlined testing phase, whereas startups might face more challenges due to evolving processes.
- **Development Model:** Agile models might require a different testing approach than Waterfall models. For example, Agile demands more flexible and iterative testing.
- **Test Approach and Tools Used:** Manual or automated testing tools can significantly impact the effort. Automation tools can reduce time in regression testing but might require more upfront effort in scripting.
- **Test Process:** A well-defined test process can lead to more accurate estimations and efficient testing.

3. **People:**

- **Skills and Experience of Team Members**: A team with experienced testers can perform more efficient and effective testing, reducing the time required.
- **Team Cohesion:** A cohesive team works better, leading to more efficient test planning and execution.

- **Leadership:** Strong leadership can streamline decision-making and test management, impacting the testing effort.
- **Domain Knowledge:** Testers with domain expertise, such as in finance or healthcare, can more quickly understand the requirements and potential issues, leading to more effective testing.

4. **Test Results:**

- **Number and Severity of Defects Found:** A high number of critical defects can significantly increase the testing effort, as it requires additional time to report, fix, and retest these issues.
- **Required Rework:** The rework necessary after initial testing rounds can also impact the overall testing effort. For example, if a significant feature must be redesigned due to usability issues, this can substantially increase the testing time.

In summary, test effort estimation is a complex process influenced by many factors ranging from the product's inherent characteristics to the testing team's skills and experience. Each factor plays a crucial role in determining the scope, approach, and duration of the testing effort required for a project.

Accurate estimation is a critical factor in achieving effective project planning and seamless execution within the ever-evolving realm of software testing. Estimations play a pivotal role at various project stages, and their level of detail and accuracy may vary accordingly. Initial estimations are essential as they set the project's foundation. Still, it is equally crucial to revisit and refine these estimations as new insights and information emerge throughout the project's lifecycle. This dynamic process ensures that estimations align with the evolving project landscape and contribute to its successful outcome.

5.1.5 Test Case Prioritization

Once the test cases and procedures have been specified and organised into test suites, the next step is creating a test execution schedule. This schedule defines the order in which the test suites will be run, considering various factors that impact the testing process.

Factors Influencing Test Execution Schedule:

1. **Prioritization:** One key consideration is the prioritisation of test cases. Test cases can be categorised and executed based on their importance or criticality. Common prioritisation strategies include:

- **Risk-based prioritisation:** This strategy orders test execution based on risk analysis results. Test cases covering the most significant risks are executed first.
- **Coverage-based prioritisation:** Test cases are executed to achieve specific coverage goals, such as statement coverage. Test cases that contribute to the highest coverage are performed first. An alternative approach, known as additional coverage prioritisation, focuses on maximising additional coverage with each subsequent test case.
- **Requirements-based prioritisation:** This strategy aligns test execution with the priorities of the requirements tied to the corresponding test cases. Stakeholders determine requirement priorities, and test cases linked to the most critical requirements are executed first.

2. **Dependencies:** The test execution order must consider any dependencies between test cases. Suppose a test case with a higher priority relies on the results of a lower-priority test case. In that case, the lower-priority test case should be executed first to provide the necessary foundation.

3. **Confirmation and Regression Tests:** Confirmation tests, which ensure that specific issues have been resolved, and regression tests,

which verify that changes have not introduced new defects, must also be prioritised within the test execution schedule.

4. **Efficiency:** Efficiency is a critical factor. Test cases should be organised to optimise the process, ensuring necessary tests are executed without delays.

5. **Resource Availability:** The availability of resources such as test tools, test environments, and personnel must be considered when creating the execution schedule. Some resources may only be available during specific time windows, which should be factored into the scheduling.

In an ideal scenario, test cases would be executed based on their priority using one of the prioritisation mentioned above strategies. However, as mentioned earlier, dependencies between test cases can sometimes complicate this process. In such cases, careful planning and coordination are required to ensure that test cases are executed in the correct order.

Ultimately, the test execution schedule plays a crucial role in the testing process, ensuring that tests are conducted efficiently and effectively, considering prioritisation, dependencies, resource availability, and the specific goals of the testing effort.

5.1.6 Test Pyramid

The concept of the Test Pyramid is a valuable model in the software testing domain. It offers insights into the varying levels of granularity that different tests may possess and guides test automation and effort allocation within a testing strategy.

Key Aspects of the Test Pyramid:

1. Different Test Granularity:

The Test Pyramid model underscores the idea that tests can have different levels of granularity. In simpler terms, some tests focus on specific, more minor aspects of the software, while others encompass more extensive, more comprehensive functionalities.

2. Support for Test Automation:

The Test Pyramid serves as a guide for teams regarding test automation. It helps teams decide which tests are best suited for automation and where to allocate their testing efforts.

3. Emphasis on Lower-Level Tests:

One fundamental principle behind the Test Pyramid is the emphasis on lower-level tests. These tests target smaller, isolated software components characterised by speed and specificity.

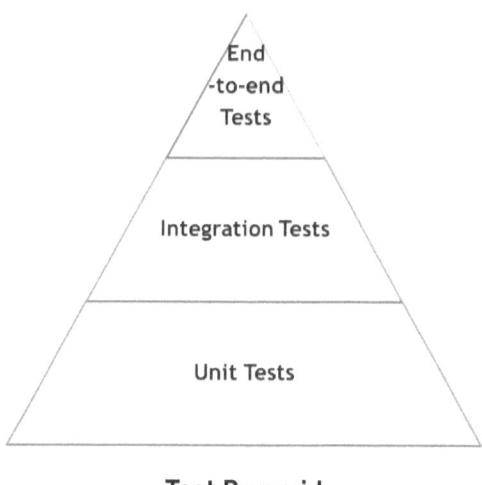

Test Pyramid

Understanding the Pyramid Layers

The Test Pyramid consists of layers, each representing a group of tests with distinct characteristics. As we ascend the layers, the granularity of the tests decreases, along with their isolation and execution time. Let's delve into the specific layers:

Bottom Layer:

- Tests in this layer are characterised by their:
- Small scope
- High degree of isolation
- Speedy execution
- Focus on specific functionality
- Due to their narrow focus, a substantial number of tests in this layer are required to achieve adequate coverage.

Top Layer:

- This layer features tests that are:
- Complex in nature
- High-level (with lower granularity and less isolation)
- End-to-end in scope
- Slower to execute
- Designed to assess a broader piece of functionality
- Fewer tests from this layer are needed to achieve comprehensive coverage due to their broader scope.

Variations in Layer Names and Numbers

The Test Pyramid model allows for flexibility in the number and names of its layers, depending on the specific testing needs and context. For instance:

- The original Test Pyramid model, proposed by Cohn in 2009, defines three layers as "unit tests," "service tests," and "UI tests."
- Another popular model categorises tests into "unit tests," "integration tests" (component integration), and "end-to-end tests."

Test Levels and Test Automation

In addition to the varying granularity at different test layers within the Test Pyramid, it also discusses the various test automation approaches used at these different test levels.

- Acceptance tests are automated using GUI (Graphical User Interface) tools.
- System tests are also automated using GUI tools.
- Integration tests, which leverage API-based tools for automation.
- Unit tests focus on specific components and are automated using API-based tools.

The Test Pyramid is valuable for structuring and optimising software testing efforts. It highlights the importance of a balanced approach to testing by incorporating various levels of granularity, from fine-grained unit tests to broader end-to-end tests, while emphasising test automation's benefits. The specific number and names of layers may vary, but the underlying principles remain consistent across different testing contexts.

5.1.7 Testing Quadrants

Brian Marick introduced the concept of testing quadrants to assist in organising various test levels and types within Agile software development. This model is a valuable tool for test management, visualising and including appropriate test types and levels within the Software Development Life Cycle (SDLC). It also helps convey the nature of tests to all stakeholders, including developers, testers, and business representatives.

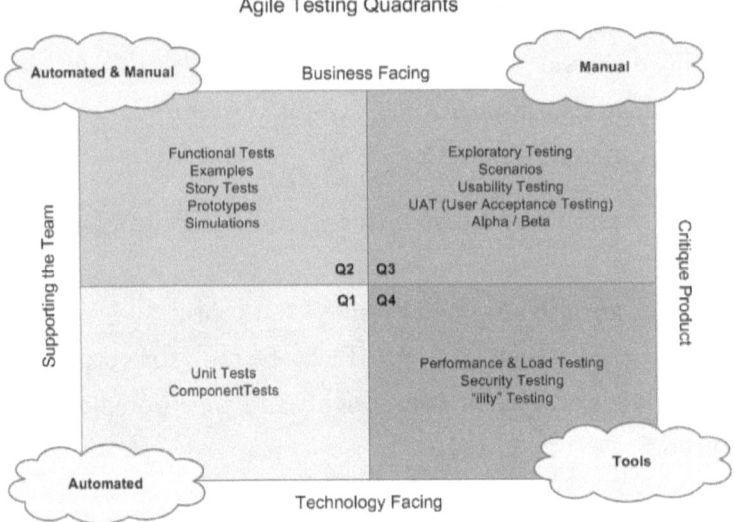

Agile Testing Quadrants

Key Characteristics of Testing Quadrants

Tests can be classified based on two key dimensions:

- **Business-facing or Technology-facing:** Tests can focus on business functionality or technical aspects.
- **Supporting the Team or Critiquing the Product:** Tests can either guide the development process or assess the product against expectations.

The Four Quadrants:

1. Quadrant Q1 (Technology-facing, Supports the Team):

- Contains tests such as component and component integration tests.
- These tests should be automated and integrated into the Continuous Integration (CI) process.
- Example: Verifying that individual software components work correctly and in harmony.

2. **Quadrant Q2 (Business-facing, Supports the Team):**

   - Encompasses a range of tests, including functional tests, examples, user story tests, user experience prototypes, API testing, and simulations.
   - These tests primarily check whether the software meets the defined acceptance criteria.
   - They can be conducted manually or automated.
   - Example: Testing whether a new feature behaves as expected in response to user interactions.

3. **Quadrant Q3 (Business-facing, Critiques the Product):**

   - Comprises tests like exploratory testing, usability testing, and user acceptance testing.
   - These tests are user-oriented and often performed manually.
   - Example: Assessing the user-friendliness of a software application through hands-on exploration.

4. **Quadrant Q4 (Technology-facing, Critiques the Product):**

   - Includes tests like smoke tests and non-functional tests, excluding usability tests.
   - Smoke tests check if the basic functionality of the software is intact.
   - Non-functional tests evaluate aspects like performance, security, and scalability.
   - These tests are typically automated.
   - Example: Ensuring a web application can handle a specified number of simultaneous users without degradation.

In essence, testing quadrants provide a structured framework for categorising and understanding the various tests in Agile software development. They help ensure that all necessary testing is conducted throughout the development process and assist in effective communication between stakeholders involved in the project.

5.2 Risk Management

In the realm of software testing, risk management plays a pivotal role in ensuring that a project stays on course and delivers successful outcomes. Let's delve into the essential aspects of risk management, its definitions, components, and practical applications.

5.2.1 Risk Definition and Risk Attributes

Defining Risk

Risk, in the context of software testing and project management, refers to potential events, hazards, threats, or situations that, if they occur, may have adverse effects. Organisations constantly face internal and external factors that introduce uncertainty into their ability to achieve objectives. Managing these risks is essential to increasing the likelihood of achieving those objectives, improving product quality, and gaining stakeholders' confidence and trust.

In simpler terms, risk could potentially lead to unfavourable consequences. It's the uncertainty that looms over project objectives.

Risk Management

Risk management is the systematic process of identifying, assessing, and controlling risks to increase the likelihood of achieving objectives, enhance product quality, and bolster stakeholders' confidence and trust.

The core activities of risk management are:

1. **Risk Analysis:** This comprises two key components: risk identification and risk assessment. Risk identification involves generating a comprehensive list of potential risks. Stakeholders can uncover risks using brainstorming, workshops, interviews, or cause-effect diagrams. Risk assessment then categorises these identified risks, determines their likelihood and impact, prioritises them, and proposes ways to

address them. You can choose between quantitative and qualitative approaches for risk assessment. The quantitative approach calculates the risk level by multiplying risk likelihood and impact. In contrast, the qualitative approach employs a risk matrix.

2. **Risk Control:** This encompasses risk mitigation and risk monitoring. Risk mitigation involves implementing actions proposed during risk assessment to reduce risk levels. The goal is to minimise the impact of identified risks. Risk monitoring ensures the effectiveness of mitigation actions, provides insights to refine risk assessment, and identifies emerging risks.

Risk-Based Testing

A key concept that stems from risk management is "risk-based testing." Risk-based testing determines, prioritises, and manages test activities based on risk analysis and control outcomes. This approach aligns testing efforts with the most significant risks, optimising resource utilisation and defect detection.

Risk Factors

Risk can be understood by considering two key factors:

1. **Risk Likelihood (probability):** This measures the probability of the risk occurring, represented as a value between zero and one.

2. **Risk Impact (consequences):** This pertains to the consequences or harm resulting from risk occurrence.

Risk Level

The product of risk likelihood and risk impact determines the overall risk level. The higher the risk level, the more critical it is and the more attention it demands.

5.2.2 Project Risks and Product Risks

In the realm of software testing, we commonly deal with two types of risks:

1. **Project Risks:** These are associated with the management and control of the testing project itself. Project risks encompass various dimensions such as organisational issues (e.g., delays in work product deliveries, inaccurate estimates, cost-cutting), people-related matters (e.g., skills shortages, conflicts, communication problems), technical challenges (e.g., scope creep, inadequate tool support), and supplier-related concerns (e.g., third-party delivery failures, supplier bankruptcy). Project risks can impact the project's schedule, budget, and scope when they materialise.

2. **Product Risks:** Also known as quality risks, these are directly linked to the quality characteristics of the software or system under test, as described in the ISO 25010 quality model. Product risks include potential issues like missing or incorrect functionality, runtime errors, architectural flaws, algorithm inefficiency, inadequate response times, poor user experiences, and security vulnerabilities. When product risks manifest, they can lead to undesirable consequences, including user dissatisfaction, revenue loss, damage to reputation, and even legal ramifications in extreme cases.

Consequences of Product Risks

The consequences of product risks can be severe and far-reaching, including:

- User dissatisfaction
- Loss of revenue, trust, and reputation
- Harm to third parties
- High maintenance costs and helpdesk overload
- Legal Penalties

- In extreme scenarios, physical harm, injuries, or even loss of life.

5.2.3 Product Risk Analysis

Product risk analysis increases awareness of product risks and guides testing efforts to minimise residual risk. It is a vital component of risk management within software testing.

Product risk analysis involves two main steps:

1. **Risk Identification:** This entails generating a comprehensive list of potential risks. Stakeholders can identify risks through various techniques and tools, such as brainstorming, workshops, interviews, or cause-effect diagrams.

2. **Risk Assessment:** Here, identified risks are categorised, and their likelihood and impact are determined. Risks are then prioritised, and strategies for handling them are proposed. Risk assessment can take a quantitative (calculating risk levels), a qualitative approach (using the risk matrix), or a combination of both.

The outcomes of product risk analysis significantly influence testing:

- Determine the scope of testing to be conducted.
- Dictate the specific test levels and types to be employed.
- Guide the selection of test techniques and coverage criteria.
- Aid in estimating the effort required for testing tasks.
- Prioritise testing to uncover critical defects early.
- Suggest additional activities beyond testing to mitigate risk.

By focusing on areas of higher risk, testing efforts become more effective in identifying and addressing potential issues.

5.2.4 Product Risk Control

Product risk control comprises the actions taken in response to identified and assessed product risks. It involves two core components:

1. **Risk Mitigation:** This phase involves implementing actions proposed during risk assessment to reduce the level of risk. It is a proactive approach to minimising potential issues.

2. **Risk Monitoring:** Risk monitoring ensures effective mitigation actions, provides additional information for refining risk assessments, and identifies emerging risks.

Response Options to Risk

Once a risk has been analysed, various response options are available:

- **Risk Mitigation by Testing** involves testing strategies to reduce product risk. Actions may include selecting testers with appropriate skills, ensuring the right level of testing independence, conducting reviews and static analysis, applying suitable test techniques and coverage levels, addressing affected quality characteristics, and performing dynamic testing, including regression testing.
- **Risk Acceptance:** Sometimes, living with a certain level of risk may be deemed acceptable without further mitigation efforts.
- **Risk Transfer:** Transferring risk to third parties, such as through insurance or contractual arrangements.
- **Contingency Plan:** Preparing a plan to manage and respond to risks if they materialise.

Actions to Mitigate Product Risks by Testing:

1. **Select Testers with Suitable Experience and Skills:** The expertise of the testing team is crucial. Testers should be chosen based on their relevant experience and skills to handle the specific challenges of the

product. For instance, a tester with a background in cybersecurity would be invaluable for a software product that takes sensitive data.

2. **Ensure an Appropriate Level of Testing Independence:** Independence in testing helps in unbiased and objective assessment of the product. This might involve having a separate quality assurance team or bringing in external testers not engaged in the development process. Such independence can lead to identifying issues that the development team might overlook.

3. **Conduct Reviews and Static Analysis:** Before dynamic testing, it's essential to review the code and conduct static analysis. This can include walkthroughs, inspections, and automated static analysis tools to detect potential issues like syntax errors, code smells, or security vulnerabilities early in the development cycle.

4. **Apply Appropriate Test Techniques and Coverage Levels:** Different test techniques, such as boundary value analysis, equivalence partitioning, or state transition testing, should be applied based on the nature of the product. Additionally, determining the right level of test coverage is crucial to ensure that all critical aspects of the product are tested without unnecessary duplication of effort.

5. **Address Affected Quality Characteristics:** It's essential to focus on specific quality characteristics most relevant to the product, such as performance, usability, reliability, and security. Tailoring the testing approach to these characteristics ensures that the product meets its quality goals and user expectations.

6. **Perform Dynamic Testing, Including Regression Testing:** Dynamic testing involves executing the software to validate its behaviour against expected results. This includes a range of tests from unit testing to system testing. Additionally, regression testing is vital whenever changes are made to the code to ensure that new updates do not adversely affect existing functionalities.

By implementing these actions, organisations can significantly enhance their ability to identify and mitigate risks associated with their products, leading to software that is functionally sound but also robust and reliable in various user scenarios.

In summary, understanding and managing risk in software testing is fundamental for ensuring the quality and success of testing projects. Risk-based testing, driven by effective risk analysis and control, enables organisations to prioritise efforts where they matter most and minimise potential negative impacts. A proactive approach to risk management provides opportunities to reduce product risks and enhance the overall testing process.

5.3 Test Monitoring, Test Control, and Test Completion

In software testing, the processes of test monitoring, control, and test completion play pivotal roles in ensuring the effectiveness and efficiency of the testing phase. Let's delve into each of these aspects and understand their significance.

Test Monitoring

Test monitoring revolves around collecting valuable information about the ongoing testing activities. This information is a compass for assessing testing progress and determining whether the predefined test exit criteria or the associated tasks align with expectations. These criteria often encompass meeting targets related to the coverage of product risks, requirements, or acceptance criteria.

Consider this scenario: During the testing phase of a software project, the team monitors the progress of test case execution. They keep track of the number of test cases executed, passed, and failed. This data allows them to assess whether they meet their predefined coverage goals and whether the test exit criteria are within reach.

Test Control

Leveraging the insights garnered from test monitoring, test control comes into play. It involves the application of control directives based on the gathered information. These directives offer guidance and prescribe corrective actions to ensure testing remains as effective and efficient as possible.

Here are some examples of control directives in action:

- **Reprioritizing Tests:** When a previously identified risk materialises, the testing team may promptly reorder their test priorities to address this new challenge.

- **Re-evaluating Test Entry/Exit Criteria:** If significant rework is performed on a particular test item, it may necessitate re-evaluating whether it still meets the entry and exit criteria.
- **Adjusting the Test Schedule:** Delays in the delivery of the test environment or other resources may require adjustments to the testing timeline.
- **Resource Allocation:** Additional resources may be allocated when and where they are needed to ensure comprehensive testing.

Imagine a scenario where the software delivery is delayed due to unforeseen circumstances. In response, the testing team reevaluates their test schedule and reprioritises specific critical tests to address the delay effectively. This agile response is an example of test control in action.

Test Completion

Test completion activities occur at significant project milestones, marking the conclusion of specific testing phases. These milestones could include the completion of a test level, the conclusion of an agile iteration, the wrapping up of an entire test project (or its cancellation), the release of a software system, or the completion of a maintenance release.

Consider a scenario where a software development project has reached its release phase. The testing team then prepares a test completion report consolidating the experiences, testware, and other relevant information gathered during testing. This report provides critical insights into the overall testing process and its outcomes.

5.3.1 Metrics Used in Testing

Metrics are an essential component of testing, providing valuable data to assess progress, quality, and the effectiveness of testing activities. Test monitoring focuses on gathering various metrics supporting test control and test completion. Let's explore some standard test metrics:

1. **Project Progress Metrics:** These metrics are essential for tracking the efficiency and effectiveness of the testing process. They include measures like the percentage of tasks completed against the planned schedule, the utilisation rate of resources, and the total effort expended in testing activities. For example, if a project is scheduled to complete 50% of its tasks by a specific date, the project progress metrics will indicate whether this target is being met.

2. **Test Progress Metrics:** These metrics focus specifically on the progress of testing activities. They include the rate of test case implementation (how quickly test cases are being prepared), the readiness status of the test environment (whether the environment is set up and configured for testing), the number of test cases executed versus those not run, and the pass/fail ratio of these test cases. For instance, many test cases not running might indicate a bottleneck in the testing process.

3. **Product Quality Metrics:** These metrics are crucial for assessing the quality of the software product. They measure aspects like system availability (how often the system is operational and accessible), response time (how quickly the system responds to user requests), and mean time to failure (the average time between system failures). These metrics help in understanding the reliability and performance of the software.

4. **Defect Metrics:** These metrics provide quantitative data on defects. This includes the total number of defects found, the number of defects fixed, defect density (defects relative to the software size), and the percentage of defects detected through testing. For example, a high defect density might indicate areas of the software that require more focused testing.

5. **Risk Metrics:** Risk metrics evaluate and quantify a project's residual risk level. They help identify areas that need more attention or where contingency plans might be required. These metrics are critical in

projects with high complexity or those necessary from a business perspective.

6. **Coverage Metrics:** Coverage metrics are vital for ensuring comprehensive testing. They measure the extent to which tests have covered the software's requirements and code. For example, a requirement coverage metric can indicate what percentage of the specified requirements have been tested, helping identify gaps in the testing process.

7. **Cost Metrics:** These metrics provide insights into the financial aspects of testing. They include the cost of conducting tests and the organisational cost of maintaining quality. This can involve direct costs like tooling and resources and indirect costs such as the time spent on rework due to defects found in testing.

These test metrics offer a detailed and multi-dimensional view of the testing process, product quality, and project health. They enable project managers and testing teams to make informed decisions, identify areas for improvement, and ensure that the project objectives are met efficiently and effectively.

Think of these metrics as the instruments on your car's dashboard, helping you gauge your progress and the overall health of your testing efforts.

5.3.2 Test Reports: Purpose, Content, and Audience

In software testing, the creation and dissemination of test reports serve as a critical link in the chain of communication and decision-making. These reports are essential for summarising and conveying test information during and after the testing phase. Let's explore these vital reports' purpose, content, and intended audience.

Purpose of Test Reports

The primary purpose of test reports is two-fold:

1. **Summarization:** They concisely summarise test activities, progress, and outcomes.

2. **Communication:** They act as a means of communicating vital information to relevant stakeholders, facilitating informed decision-making.

Content of Test Reports

1. Test Progress Reports

Test progress reports are instrumental in ensuring the ongoing control of the testing process. To effectively support this control, they must contain sufficient information for stakeholders to adjust the test schedule, allocate resources judiciously, or modify the test plan when circumstances deviate from the initial plan. These reports are typically generated at regular intervals, which can vary from daily to weekly.

Key components of test progress reports include:

- **Test Period:** Indicating the timeframe covered by the report.
- **Test Progress:** Highlighting whether testing is progressing ahead of schedule, on track, or falling behind. Notable deviations from the plan are also outlined.
- **Impediments for Testing:** Identifying any obstacles or challenges encountered during testing and providing insights into the workarounds used to address them.
- **Test Metrics:** Drawing from the metrics discussed in Section 5.3.1 (e.g., progress in test case implementation, test environment readiness, test execution results).
- **New and Changed Risks:** Detailing any risks that have emerged or evolved during the testing period.
- **Testing Planned for the Next Period:** Outlining the testing activities scheduled for the upcoming phase.

2. Test Completion Reports

Test completion reports are prepared when a project, test level, or specific test type reaches its conclusion, ideally meeting its predefined exit criteria. These reports serve as comprehensive summaries of the entire testing endeavour.

Key elements of test completion reports encompass:

- **Test Summary:** Providing an overview of the testing activities conducted, their outcomes, and the overall quality of the product under test.
- **Testing and Product Quality Evaluation:** Assessing testing against the original test plan, including test objectives and exit criteria.
- **Deviations from the Test Plan:** Highlight discrepancies between the planned schedule, duration, effort, and actual results.
- **Testing Impediments and Workarounds:** Documenting challenges faced during testing and the strategies employed to overcome them.
- **Test Metrics:** Drawing from the data captured in the test progress reports to provide a holistic view of the testing process.
- **Unmitigated Risks and Unresolved Defects:** Enumerating unaddressed risks and defects that have not yet been fixed.
- **Lessons Learned:** Sharing insights and experiences relevant to future testing efforts, promoting continuous improvement.

Audience for Test Reports

The intended audience for test reports can vary depending on the nature and stage of testing. Stakeholders require different levels of detail, formality, and frequency in reporting. Here are some considerations:

- **Internal Team Members:** Reporting on test progress to members of the same team is often frequent and informal. It involves regular updates and discussions to keep everyone on the same page.

- **External Stakeholders:** A more formal and structured approach is adopted when reporting on testing for a completed project or a specific milestone. Reports follow predefined templates and occur less frequently, typically at project milestones.
- **Regulatory and Compliance Authorities:** In some cases, compliance with industry standards or regulatory bodies may necessitate specific reporting formats and frequencies.
- **Management:** Reports provided to management may focus on high-level summaries and key performance indicators (KPIs) to aid strategic decision-making.

The formality, detail, and frequency level should align with each audience group's needs and expectations.

For standardised templates and examples of test progress reports (referred to as test status reports) and test completion reports, the ISO/IEC/IEEE 29119-3 standard serves as a valuable reference.

In essence, test reports are the bridge connecting the testing process with stakeholders. This facilitates effective communication and informed decision-making, ultimately contributing to the success of software testing endeavours.

5.3.3 Communicating the Status of Testing

The way test status is communicated varies based on factors such as test management concerns, organisational test strategies, and regulatory standards. Several options are available for conveying test status, each catering to specific needs:

- **Verbal Communication:** Direct discussions with team members and stakeholders.
- **Dashboards:** Visualization tools like CI/CD, task boards, and burn-down charts.

- **Electronic Communication Channels:** Utilization of mediums such as email and chat.
- **Online Documentation:** Posting updates in a shared online repository.
- **Formal Test Reports:** Structured reports that follow predefined templates.

For instance, formal communication channels like online documentation or structured reports may be preferred in a globally distributed team, where face-to-face communication is challenging due to geographical distances and time differences.

In conclusion, test monitoring, control, completion, and judicious use of metrics and effective test reporting form the bedrock of successful testing endeavours. These practices ensure that software testing remains on track, adapts to changing circumstances, and communicates its status effectively to stakeholders, ultimately contributing to delivering high-quality software products.

5.4 Configuration Management

Configuration management (CM) is a vital discipline in testing, pivotal in identifying, controlling, and tracking various work products crucial for effective testing. These work products include test plans, test strategies, test conditions, test cases, test scripts, test results, test logs, and test reports, all treated as configuration items.

In a complex configuration item, such as a test environment, CM maintains records of the item itself and its components, their interrelationships, and their respective versions. When a configuration item is approved for testing, it attains a baseline status. Once established as a baseline, any modifications to the item can only be made through a formal change control process.

One of the key functions of configuration management is to keep a meticulous record of changes made to configuration items when a new baseline is created. This historical data enables the ability to revert to a previous baseline when needed, facilitating the reproduction of prior test results.

To effectively support the testing process, configuration management ensures the following:

1. **Unique Identification:** Every configuration item, including individual parts of the test object known as test items, is uniquely identified. This helps in distinguishing between different items and their versions.

2. **Version Control:** CM ensures that versions of configuration items are systematically controlled. This means that changes to these items are carefully managed, allowing for a clear understanding of how they evolve.

3. **Traceability:** Configuration management establishes and maintains traceability between configuration items. This traceability ensures that

relationships between various elements are well-documented, enabling a comprehensive understanding of the testing process.

4. **Baselining:** Configuration management plays a pivotal role in supporting the concept of baselining. Baselining involves setting a reference point or benchmark, typically representing a stable and approved configuration of items. CM helps control access to these baselines, ensuring they remain consistent and reliable throughout the testing process.

When planning for testing, it is essential to establish configuration management procedures and infrastructure. This step is critical for maintaining the integrity and consistency of components, systems, and testware used in the testing process.

In contemporary software development practices, especially in the context of DevOps, continuous integration, continuous delivery, continuous deployment, and the associated testing are typically implemented as part of an automated DevOps pipeline. Configuration management is an integral component in such automated pipelines, ensuring that all necessary configuration items are correctly managed and version-controlled to support the software's rapid and reliable deployment.

Configuration management is essential in testing, guaranteeing the integrity of various components, systems, and testware. It is crucial for maintaining consistency, traceability, and controlled access to configuration items throughout the testing process, including its integration into automated DevOps pipelines.

5.5 Defects Management

In software testing, the quest for perfection often starts with recognising that defects are integral to the development process. To effectively manage defects, a well-defined defect management process is indispensable. Although we often refer to these issues as "defects," it's important to note that they might be something different, such as false positives or change requests. Resolution of their true nature occurs during the defect management process.

Defect Reporting Across the SDLC

Anomalies, which could be defects, surface at various stages of the Software Development Life Cycle (SDLC), and their format depends on the specific phase they emerge in. At the very least, the defect management process includes a structured workflow for handling individual anomalies, starting from their discovery and leading to their eventual closure. It also incorporates rules for classifying these anomalies.

The workflow typically encompasses the following activities:

1. Logging the reported anomalies.
2. Analysing and classifying them.
3. Deciding on an appropriate response, whether fixing the issue or leaving it as is.
4. Closing the defect report.

Crucially, this process is followed by all stakeholders involved in the development and testing efforts. In addition, it's advisable to apply similar defect management principles to issues arising from static testing, mainly static analysis.

Objectives of Defect Reports:

Defect reports serve several essential objectives:

1. Providing those responsible for resolving defects with comprehensive information to facilitate resolution.
2. Offering a means to track the quality of the work product.
3. Generating insights for the improvement of both development and testing processes.

Defect Reports during Dynamic Testing

A typical defect report created during dynamic testing includes the following components:

- A unique identifier.
- A title with a summary of the reported anomaly.
- The date when the anomaly was observed and details about the issuing organisation and the author (including their role).
- Identification of the test object and the test environment.
- Contextual information about the defect (e.g., the test case being executed, the test activity underway, the SDLC phase, and other pertinent details such as the testing technique, checklist, or test data in use).
- A description of the failure aimed at enabling reproduction and resolution. This description should encompass the anomaly detection steps and any relevant test logs, database dumps, screenshots, or recordings.
- The expected results versus the actual results.
- An assessment of the severity of the defect in terms of its impact on stakeholder interests or requirements.
- A priority level indicating the urgency of addressing the defect.
- The current status of the defect (e.g., open, deferred, duplicate, waiting for resolution, awaiting confirmation testing, re-opened, closed, or rejected).
- References, including any relevant test cases.

It's worth noting that specific defect management tools may automatically include and manage certain details of defect reports, such as assigning a unique identifier and updating the defect report's status as it progresses through the workflow.

False Positive and False Negative Explained

A **False Positive** is an erroneous outcome that arises when a test result, statistical inference, or decision implies a positive occurrence of a condition, attribute, or event when, in fact, it is not present. However, a false positive occurs when a test or analysis incorrectly indicates a problem or condition, even though there is no such problem or condition.

Conversely, a **False Negative** occurs when a test result, statistical conclusion, or decision suggests a negative occurrence of a condition, attribute, or event when, in reality, it is indeed present. In straightforward terms, a false negative arises when a test or analysis wrongly shows no problem or condition when, in truth, a problem or condition exists.

Handling Non-Defect Anomalies

In the defect investigation process, testers must also be vigilant in identifying non-defect anomalies, particularly false positives. False positives occur when a test or analysis suggests a problem or condition that does not exist.

The management of defects is a pivotal aspect of the software testing process. It involves the identification and resolution of issues and the meticulous tracking and documentation of these anomalies. This structured approach ensures that software quality is upheld and provides valuable insights for process improvement. The ISO/IEC/IEEE 29119-3 standard offers templates and examples of defect reports, which it refers to as incident reports, to guide practitioners in this critical endeavour.

Summary

Test Planning: A crucial phase in software testing, guiding the process from start to finish. It includes documenting objectives, achieving test objectives, ensuring compliance, communication, and adherence to test policy and strategy.

Test Plan - Purpose and Content:

- **Purpose:** To outline aims, resources, and processes, ensure compliance, facilitate communication, and adhere to test policy.
- **Content:** Includes the context of testing, assumptions and constraints, stakeholders, communication strategies, risk register, test approach, and budget and schedule.

Test Strategy and Approaches: High-level description of testing methods and practical steps for specific projects or releases.

Planning in Agile Projects:

- **Release Planning:** High-level planning for delivering functionality over iterations.
- **Iteration Planning:** Detailed planning within each iteration.

Entry and Exit Criteria: Define conditions for starting and concluding testing activities.

Test Effort Estimations: Predicting the effort required for testing using metrics-based and expert-based estimation techniques.

Test Case Prioritization: Scheduling test cases based on prioritisation, dependencies, and resource availability.

Test Pyramid: A model for structuring test efforts, emphasising lower-level tests and differentiating between test granularity levels.

Testing Quadrants: Introduced by Brian Marick, this concept helps organise test levels and types in Agile development.

Risk Management in Software Testing: Involves identifying, assessing, and controlling risks to enhance product quality and stakeholder confidence.

Test Monitoring, Control, and Completion: These processes ensure testing effectiveness, collect and analyse metrics, and summarise outcomes at project milestones.

Communicating the Status of Testing: Involves verbal communication, dashboards, electronic channels, and formal reports to convey test status.

Configuration Management for Testing: Manages various testing work products, ensuring consistency and controlled access.

Defects Management: A process for handling defects throughout the SDLC, including reporting and tracking.

This chapter provides a comprehensive overview of managing testing activities, covering aspects from test planning and strategy to risk management, monitoring, and defect management. It emphasises the importance of structured processes and effective communication in ensuring the success of software testing endeavours.

Quiz 5

1. In Agile software development, release planning is a low-level planning activity focusing on delivering specific user stories or features within a single iteration. (True/False)
2. A test plan's purpose includes ensuring compliance with established criteria and communicating among team members and stakeholders. (True/False)
3. The Test Pyramid model suggests more high-level tests than lower-level tests. (True/False)
4. Risk-based testing aligns testing efforts with the most significant risks to optimise resource utilisation and defect detection. (True/False)
5. Test cases in the Test Pyramid's bottom layer are characterised by their complex nature and high-level scope. (True/False)
6. In software testing, configuration management is only concerned with managing test cases and test scripts. (True/False)
7. Entry criteria in software testing are the set of prerequisites that must be satisfied before concluding a specific testing activity. (True/False)
8. Test effort estimations become more accurate as the task scale increases. (True/False)
9. In defect management, a false positive occurs when a test incorrectly indicates the absence of a problem or condition. (True/False)
10. Test monitoring involves applying control directives based on information gathered about ongoing testing activities. (True/False)

Quiz 5: Answers

1. **In Agile software development, release planning is a low-level planning activity focusing on delivering specific user stories or features within a single iteration. (False)**

    - Justification: In Agile software development, release planning is a high-level planning activity that focuses on delivering valuable increments of functionality, typically spanning multiple iterations.

2. **A test plan's purpose includes ensuring compliance with established criteria and communicating among team members and stakeholders. (True)**

    - Justification: One key objectives of a test plan is to ensure that test activities align with established criteria and to facilitate communication among team members and stakeholders.

3. **The Test Pyramid model suggests more high-level tests than lower-level tests. (False)**

    - Justification: The Test Pyramid model emphasises the importance of having a more significant number of lower-level tests (like unit tests) compared to fewer high-level tests (like end-to-end tests).

4. **Risk-based testing aligns testing efforts with the most significant risks to optimise resource utilisation and defect detection. (True)**

    - Justification: Risk-based testing is an approach that prioritises and manages test activities based on risk analysis outcomes, focusing on significant risks to optimise testing efforts.

5. **Test cases in the Test Pyramid's bottom layer are characterised by their complex nature and high-level scope. (False)**

- Justification: Tests in the bottom layer of the Test Pyramid are characterised by their small scope, high isolation, speedy execution, and focus on specific functionality.

6. **In software testing, configuration management is only concerned with managing test cases and test scripts. (False)**

    - Justification: Configuration management in software testing involves identifying, controlling, and tracking various work products, including test plans, test strategies, test conditions, test cases, test scripts, test results, test logs, and test reports.

7. **Entry criteria in software testing are the set of prerequisites that must be satisfied before concluding a specific testing activity. (False)**

    - Justification: Entry criteria, also known as preconditions, are the prerequisites that must be satisfied before commencing a specific testing activity. Exit criteria define the conditions to conclude a testing activity.

8. **Test effort estimations become more accurate as the task scale increases. (False)**

    - Justification: Estimation accuracy typically diminishes as the task scale increases. Breaking down large tasks into smaller sub-tasks can enhance estimation accuracy.

9. **In defect management, a false positive occurs when a test incorrectly indicates the absence of a problem or condition. (False)**

    - Justification: A false positive is an erroneous outcome where a test incorrectly indicates the presence of a problem or condition when it is not present. The opposite, a false negative, occurs when a test wrongly shows the absence of a problem or condition.

10. **Test monitoring involves applying control directives based on information gathered about ongoing testing activities. (False)**

    - Justification: Test monitoring collects information on the ongoing testing activities. Test control, on the other hand, involves applying control directives based on the gathered information to ensure testing remains effective and efficient.

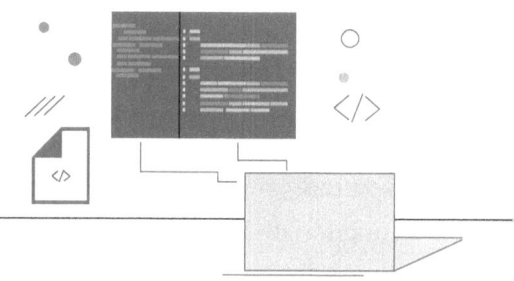

CHAPTER 6

TEST TOOLS

(2 QUESTIONS | 20 MINUTES)

Learning Objectives for Chapter 6

6.1 Tool Support for Testing

- FL-6.1.1 (K2) Explain how different types of test tools support testing

6.2 Benefits and Risks of Test Automation

- FL-6.2.1 (K1) Recall the benefits and risks of test automation

6.1 Tool Support for Testing

Test tools are indispensable in modern software testing, offering a range of functionalities that significantly boost efficiency and quality throughout the software development lifecycle (SDLC). These tools streamline various testing activities and ensure thoroughness and accuracy in the testing process. Here's an overview of the different types of test tools and their roles:

1. **Management Tools:** These tools are pivotal in optimising the test process. They handle various SDLC aspects, including requirements, tests, defects, and configurations. For example, a tool like JIRA can be used for tracking defects, and a tool like DOORs can manage test cases.

2. **Static Testing Tools:** These assist testers in conducting reviews and static analysis, which is crucial for early defect detection. Before it's executed, tools like SonarQube, Polyspace, LDRA, and Lint tool can analyse code for potential bugs and vulnerabilities.

3. **Test Design and Implementation Tools:** These tools streamline the creation of test cases, test data, and test procedures. They make the preparation phase of testing more efficient and less prone to errors. TestRail, Testcollab, pairWise Tool, Kualitee, Datamaker, and BenderRBT can help organise and manage test cases.

4. **Test Execution and Coverage Tools:** Automation is key in modern testing, and these tools enable automated test execution and measuring test coverage. This ensures that all parts of the application are tested. Selenium, for instance, is widely used to automate web applications for testing purposes.

5. **Non-functional Testing Tools:** Certain tests, especially non-functional ones like performance or security testing, can be challenging or even impossible to perform manually. Tools like LoadRunner for

performance testing or OWASP ZAP for security testing come into play here.

6. **DevOps Tools:** These tools support DevOps's continuous integration and deployment (CI/CD) aspects. They facilitate automated build processes and workflow tracking. Jenkins is a famous example known for its ability to integrate various stages of the DevOps lifecycle.

7. **Collaboration Tools:** Effective communication is crucial in testing. Tools such as instant messaging, audio and video calling, and desktop sharing facilitate collaboration. Slack or Microsoft Teams help maintain a seamless information flow among team members.

8. **Tools for Scalability and Deployment Standardization**: With the increasing need for scalable and standardised deployment processes, tools like Docker (for containerisation) and various virtual machine platforms play a critical role.

9. **Other Testing Tools:** Any tool that aids the testing process falls under this category. For instance, spreadsheets might be used for tracking test results or planning test scenarios.

Testing teams can significantly enhance their productivity and effectiveness by incorporating these diverse test tools into their workflows. These tools simplify complex tasks and ensure that the software products meet the highest standards of quality and reliability.

6.2 Benefits and Risks of Test Automation

Automated testing tools are not a one-stop solution for success. They require a significant investment in time and effort to yield substantial and enduring benefits. This includes the introduction of the tool, its maintenance, and necessary training. Additionally, there are risks associated with automated testing that must be carefully analysed and mitigated.

Benefits of Automated Testing:

1. **Efficiency Enhancement:** Automated testing saves time by eliminating repetitive manual tasks. This includes running regression tests, re-entering test data, comparing expected versus actual results, and ensuring adherence to coding standards.

2. **Consistency and Error Prevention:** Automation enhances consistency and repeatability in testing. They also provide more accurate results, eliminating human errors. For example, tests are consistently derived from requirements, test data is systematically created, and tests are executed uniformly.

3. **Objective Assessment:** Automated tools can provide more objective assessments, such as coverage, and generate complex measures that are difficult for humans to compute.

4. **Improved Test Management:** Automation facilitates access to testing information, supporting test management and reporting through statistics, graphs, and aggregated data on test progress, defect rates, and test execution duration.

5. **Reduced Execution Time:** Automation leads to quicker test execution, enabling earlier defect detection, faster feedback, and accelerated time to market.

6. **Frees up Testers:** Automation or tools free up time for testers to focus on creating new, more in-depth, and effective tests or perform manual experience-based testing, such as exploratory testing.

Risks of Automated Testing:

1. **Unrealistic Expectations:** People can overestimate the tool's benefits, functionality, and ease of use.

2. **Resource Underestimation:** Often, the time, costs, and effort required to introduce and maintain the tool and modify existing manual test processes are underestimated.

3. **Inappropriate Use:** There are scenarios where manual testing may be more suitable than automated testing.

4. **Over-reliance on Tools:** Excessive dependence on tools can lead to neglecting the need for human critical thinking in testing. If we rely too much on automation and neglect necessary manual tests, it poses a risk.

5. **Vendor Dependency:** Risks include the vendor going out of business, discontinuing the tool, selling it, or providing inadequate support.

6. **Open-source Software Risks:** Open-source tools may be abandoned, leading to a lack of updates or requiring frequent updates due to ongoing development.

7. **Compatibility Issues:** The tool may not be compatible with the development platform.

8. **Regulatory Non-Compliance**: It can be problematic to select a tool that does not meet regulatory requirements or safety standards.

In summary, while automated testing offers significant benefits in efficiency, consistency, and enhanced test management, it also comes with challenges that require careful consideration and management. The key is to balance the advantages with a realistic understanding of the challenges to maximise the effectiveness of automated testing tools.

Summary

Chapter 6 delves into the critical role of test tools in enhancing efficiency and quality in software testing. These tools are essential in the modern software development lifecycle (SDLC), offering functionalities that streamline testing activities and ensure accuracy.

1. **Types of Test Tools:**

- **Management Tools:** Essential for optimising the test process and handling requirements, tests, defects, and configurations (e.g., JIRA, DOORs).
- **Static Testing Tools:** Aid early defect detection through reviews and static analysis (e.g., SonarQube, Polyspace).
- **Test Design and Implementation Tools:** Facilitate efficient test case creation and management (e.g., TestRail, Testcollab).
- **Test Execution and Coverage Tools:** Enable automated test execution and measure test coverage (e.g., Selenium).
- **Non-functional Testing Tools:** Crucial for performance or security testing (e.g., LoadRunner, OWASP ZAP).
- **DevOps Tools:** Support CI/CD aspects, automating build processes (e.g., Jenkins).
- **Collaboration Tools:** Enhance communication among team members (e.g., Slack, Microsoft Teams).
- **Scalability and Deployment Tools:** Address the need for scalable processes (e.g., Docker).
- **Other Testing Tools:** Include various aids like spreadsheets for test tracking.

2. **Advantages of Automated Testing:**

- Enhances efficiency by reducing manual, repetitive tasks.
- Increases consistency and prevents errors.
- Provides objective assessments and complex measures.

- Improves test management with accessible information.
- Reduces test execution time, leading to faster feedback.
- Frees up time for more in-depth test design.

3. Challenges of Automated Testing:

- Unrealistic expectations about tool benefits.
- Underestimation of resources needed for tool introduction and maintenance.
- Inappropriate use or over-reliance on tools.
- Risks associated with vendor dependency and open-source software.
- Compatibility issues and regulatory non-compliance.

In conclusion, test tools play a pivotal role in enhancing the productivity and effectiveness of testing teams. However, it's crucial to balance the benefits with a realistic understanding of the challenges to maximise the effectiveness of these tools in automated testing.

Quiz 6

1. Tool implementation requires a mature software development process. (True/False)
2. Requirement management tool is used for gathering requirements. (True/False)
3. The test comparator is mainly built into a test execution tool. (True/False)
4. Any problem in software development can be solved by using tools. (True/False)
5. Jenkins is a DevOps tool that supports continuous integration and deployment. (True/False)
6. One of the main benefits of using tools is the reduction of repetitive work. (True/False)
7. Static testing tools are used during the execution phase of code to identify bugs and vulnerabilities. (True/False)
8. Tools for facilitating the review process fall in the category of static testing tools. (True/False)
9. Defect management is often a part of a test execution tool. (True/False)

Quiz 6: Answers

1. **Tool implementation requires a mature software development process. (True)**

   - Justification: You can develop stable tools with a mature software development process. A mature process ensures the tools are implemented effectively, aligning with the development needs and maintaining stability in the software development lifecycle.

2. **Requirement management tool is used for gathering requirements. (True)**

   - Justification: This is the proper purpose of the requirement management tools. These tools are designed to gather, manage, and track requirements throughout development, ensuring that all stakeholder needs are captured and addressed.

3. **The test comparator is mainly built into a test execution tool. (True)**

   - Justification: This statement is true. A test comparator, which compares expected and actual outcomes, is often a feature integrated within test execution tools to facilitate automated testing and result analysis.

4. **Any problem in software development can be solved by using tools. (False)**

   - Justification: Tools will help find more bugs in less time, but this will not solve any issues. Tools aid the development process but cannot address every problem, especially those related to design, requirements, or strategy.

5. **Jenkins is a DevOps tool that supports continuous integration and deployment. (True)**

   - Justification: Jenkins is mentioned explicitly as a tool for integrating various DevOps lifecycle stages, including continuous integration and deployment. It automates parts of the software development process, enhancing efficiency and consistency.

6. **One of the main benefits of using tools is the reduction of repetitive work. (True)**

   - Justification: Tools help to increase efficiency by automating repetitive tasks. They streamline processes, reduce manual effort, and minimise the likelihood of human error in repetitive tasks.

7. **Static testing tools are used during the execution phase of code to identify bugs and vulnerabilities. (False)**

   - Justification: Static testing tools, like SonarQube and Lint, are used for static analysis before the code is executed, not during the execution phase. They analyse code without running it to identify potential issues.

8. **Tools for facilitating the review process fall in the category of static testing tools. (True)**

   - Justification: Under static testing tools, tools support the review process and static analysis. These tools help examine the source code or other documentation without executing the program.

9. **Defect management is often a part of a test execution tool. (False)**

   - Justification: Defect Management tools are Management Tools, not Test Execution tools. They are specialised tools for tracking and managing defects independently from the test execution process.

CHAPTER X

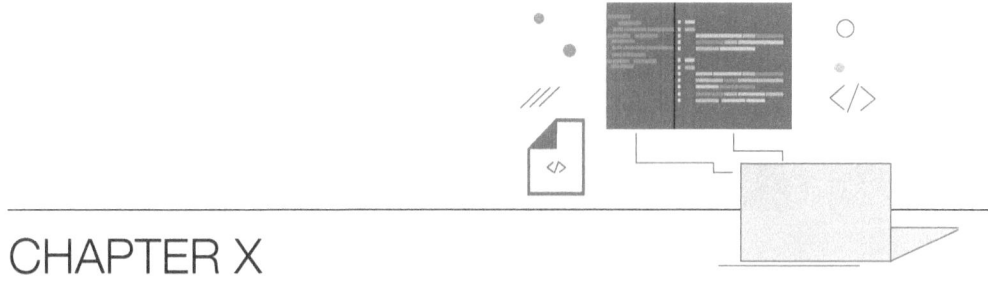

SAMPLE EXAM

1. Which of the following is an example of why testing is necessary?
   A. To directly involve a representative set of users in the development project.
   B. To meet contractual and legal requirements.
   C. To replace the need for debugging activities.
   D. To reduce project management overhead.

2. Which of the following is NOT an advantage of the whole team approach?
   A. Improved communication between team members.
   B. Improved team dynamics.
   C. The team can leverage the benefit of having needed skills inside the team.
   D. Reduced collaboration with external business users.

3. "Often, people and organisations use Testing and Quality Assurance (QA) as synonyms".
   Is the above statement correct or not? Choose the correct understanding.
   A. Not correct. Testing is super set and includes both Quality Assurance (QA) and Quality Control (QC).
   B. Not correct. Testing is a product-oriented approach aimed at identifying and correcting defects, while QA is a process-oriented approach centred on preventing issues before they arise.

C. Correct. Testing and QA are the same.

D. Correct. These names can be used interchangeably because testing and QA focus on process-related quality issues.

4. The end users are reporting many production defects in one particular functionality. It was analysed by the managers that equal test effort is being applied to all modules while every module has a different level of complexity. Complex modules have more defects in them, but most of them remain undetected as testing those modules is also very complex.

   Which of the following 'principles of testing' is NOT addressed in the above scenario?

   A. Tests wear out

   B. Absence-of-defects fallacy

   C. Early testing saves time and money

   D. Defects cluster together

5. What is a key aspect of the test execution process?

   A. Planning of automated testing methods and writing scripts.

   B. Comparison of predicted and actual outcomes.

   C. Exclusion of continuous testing practices.

   D. Ignoring the logging of test results.

6. When considering the impact of context on the test process in software development, which of the following accurately represents how contextual factors influence the choice of test strategy, techniques, and automation level?

   A. The choice of test strategy is influenced solely by technical factors such as product architecture and technology used, while the software development lifecycle determines test techniques and automation levels.

B. Stakeholders' needs, team skills, and organisational factors predominantly determine the test strategy, whereas technical factors and project constraints influence the choice of test techniques and automation level.
C. The software development lifecycle and tools available are the primary determinants of the test strategy and the degree of test automation, with little to no influence from other contextual factors.
D. Contextual factors, including stakeholders' expectations, business domain, technical factors, and organisational structure, collectively influence the test strategy, techniques, and level of automation, rather than any single factor being predominant.

7. Which of the following explains the relation between Traceability, Test Basis and Testware?
   A. Test Case traceable to the requirement calculates the residual risk in the test object.
   B. Traceability enables the assessment of test case coverage of requirements and residual risk evaluation through test results.
   C. Test Cases linked to test results directly assess the test object's compliance with requirements.
   D. Traceability is primarily used for reporting defects and has no relation to requirement coverage or risk assessment.

8. Given the following benefits and drawbacks of the independence of testing:

i. Testers and developers operate in separate locations.
ii. Testers challenge the assumptions made by programmers during code development.
iii. There is a confrontational relationship between testers and developers.

iv. Developers believe that testers bear the primary responsibility for ensuring quality.
v. Testers possess biases that differ from those of the developers.

Which are MOST likely to be considered as benefits and which are as drawbacks?

A. i, iv are benefits ii, iii, v are drawbacks
B. ii, v are benefits i, iii, iv are drawbacks
C. i, iii, iv are benefits ii, v are drawbacks
D. ii, iii, v are benefits i, iv are drawbacks

9. Which of the following is to be considered good practice for testing?
   A. There is a corresponding test activity after every software development activity.
   B. Each test level serves a specific test objective, reducing duplicity in testing activities
   C. Testing can adhere to the principle of later testing.
   D. Testers are involved in reviewing work products as soon as the final version of the documentation is available

10. In Test-Driven Development (TDD), Acceptance Test-Driven Development (ATDD), and Behaviour-Driven Development (BDD), when are tests typically defined in relation to the code?
    A. After the code is written
    B. Simultaneously with writing the code
    C. Before the code is written
    D. During code review sessions

11. Which attributes distinguish test levels and prevent overlapping test activities?
    A. Test report, Test basis, and Approach and responsibilities
    B. Test objectives, Defects and failures, and Approach and responsibilities
    C. Test cases, Defects and failures, and Approach and responsibilities

D. Test object, Test plan, and Test basis

12. In the context of software testing, how do confirmation testing and regression testing differ in their objectives and applications?
    A. Confirmation testing and regression testing both aim to confirm that an original defect has been successfully fixed, with no significant difference in their execution.
    B. Confirmation testing is performed to verify a specific defect fix, whereas regression testing is conducted to ensure that recent changes have not adversely affected existing functionalities.
    C. Regression testing is exclusively used for checking new features, while confirmation testing is restricted to verifying environmental changes.
    D. Both confirmation testing and regression testing focus on new feature enhancements, with confirmation testing being more extensive and including impact analysis.

13. How does the software development lifecycle model choice impact a software project's testing process?
    A. The SDLC model has no significant impact on testing, as testing activities remain constant regardless of the development approach.
    B. In sequential development models, dynamic testing is typically performed early in the SDLC, whereas, in Agile development, extensive prior test analysis and design are required.
    C. In iterative and incremental models, testing is limited to static methods only, while Agile development focuses on lightweight documentation without the need for test automation.
    D. In sequential development models, dynamic testing occurs later in the SDLC. In contrast, iterative and Agile models allow for both static and dynamic testing throughout, with Agile favouring lightweight documentation and extensive test automation.

14. What is a key consideration for the shift-left approach in software development?
    A. It requires minimal training and effort early in the process.
    B. It is expected to save efforts and costs earlier in the process.
    C. It involves additional training, effort, and costs earlier in the process but is anticipated to save efforts and costs later.
    D. Stakeholder buy-in is not crucial for the success of the shift-left approach.

15. Which of the following is NOT an appropriate work product for static testing techniques?
    A. Requirement specification documents.
    B. Test cases and test plans.
    C. Third-party executable code that is legally restricted from analysis.
    D. Source code.

16. In a software review process, which principal role is responsible for ensuring the effective running of review meetings, including mediation, time management, and creating a safe review environment for open discussions?
    A. Manager
    B. Author
    C. Moderator (Facilitator)
    D. Scribe (Recorder)

17. What is the primary value of static testing in the software development lifecycle?
    A. Static testing primarily enhances the graphical user interface design and improves user experience.
    B. The value of static testing lies in its ability to detect defects in the earliest phases of the SDLC, improve communication among

stakeholders, and reduce overall project costs by identifying defects that are not detectable by dynamic testing.

C. Static testing is mainly used for performance optimisation in the final stages of the SDLC.

D. The main purpose of static testing is to replace dynamic testing in later stages of the SDLC to speed up the release process.

18. Which review type is the most formal and follows a complete generic process, with the main objective being to find the maximum number of anomalies while also collecting metrics for process improvement?
    A. Informal review
    B. Walkthrough
    C. Technical Review
    D. Inspection

19. Which test technique is primarily based on the specified behaviour of the test object without considering its internal structure, making test cases independent of software implementation changes?
    A. White-box testing
    B. Experience-based testing
    C. Black-box testing
    D. Structure-based testing

20. What is the primary goal of branch testing in software testing?
    A. To achieve 100% statement coverage in the code.
    B. To design test cases that exercise branches until an acceptable level of coverage is reached.
    C. To identify defects requiring the execution of specific code paths.
    D. To measure the number of nodes in the control flow graph.

21. Which statement about the value of white-box testing is FALSE?
    A. White-box testing considers the entire software implementation, including internal logic.

B. It is effective even when the software specification is vague or outdated.
C. White-box testing relies solely on the software specification for defect detection.
D. It provides an objective measurement of code coverage.

22. The program accepts two numbers from -100 to 100 and uses them in various arithmetic calculations.

    Which of the following test techniques is more likely to detect divide-by-zero errors resulting from these inputs?
    A. Boundary Value Analysis
    B. Equivalence Partitioning
    C. Error Guessing
    D. Black Box Testing

23. Which statement regarding Exploratory Testing is NOT accurate?
    A. Exploratory testing follows predefined test cases and steps.
    B. It is particularly valuable when the test object has limited or inadequate specifications.
    C. Testers engage in simultaneous test design, execution, and evaluation to understand the test object better.
    D. Exploratory testing can be structured using session-based testing with defined time-boxes.

24. In Behaviour-Driven Development (BDD), which structure is typically used for writing scenario-oriented acceptance criteria?
    A. Start/Action/Result
    B. Cause/Effect/Resolution
    C. Given/When/Then
    D. Condition/Process/Outcome

25. A company has initiated a wellness scheme linked to its health insurance policy. The scheme's guidelines are:
    1. Employees who exercise for at least 150 minutes a week receive a $20 discount on their health insurance.
    2. Employees undergoing annual health check-ups are awarded a $15 discount.
    3. Employees who do not consume alcohol receive an additional $30 discount.

    How many test cases are required to ensure complete coverage of the equivalence partitions for valid input parameters when applying the equivalence partitioning testing technique to this scenario?
    A. 2 test cases
    B. 3 test cases
    C. 4 test cases
    D. 5 test cases

26. A system requires that the temperature setting must always be within a range of 15 to 25 degrees Celsius (both 15 and 25 are valid within the range). Which of the following represents the minimal set of tests for two-point boundary value analysis?
    A. A set of tests where the temperature is set to -5, 15, 20, and 30 degrees Celsius.
    B. A set of tests where the temperature is set to 14, 15, and 26 degrees Celsius.
    C. A set of tests where the temperature is set to 15, 18, and 25 degrees Celsius.
    D. A set of tests where the temperature is set to 14, 15, 25, and 26 degrees Celsius.

27. The RiskEvaluator tool calculates the risk associated with approving a loan for a customer based on four criteria, which the user selects from dropdown menus.

The criteria include:
- Age, with options being:
  - under 18
  - 18 to 35
  - 36 to 65
  - over 65
- Education level, with options being:
  - elementary or high school
  - undergraduate
  - graduate
- Place of residence, with options being:
  - city
  - village

When a user selects "under 18" for age, the "education" field automatically defaults to "elementary or high school" and cannot be altered. The application's final assessment categorises the risk as either:
- Low risk
- Medium risk
- High risk

What is the total number of columns in the decision table for this scenario?

A. 22
B. 24
C. 7
D. 20

28. A system implemented in an electronic gadget allows displaying the time or date, depending on the user's choice.

The accompanying state transition diagram illustrates the various states and input requests pertinent to this gadget.

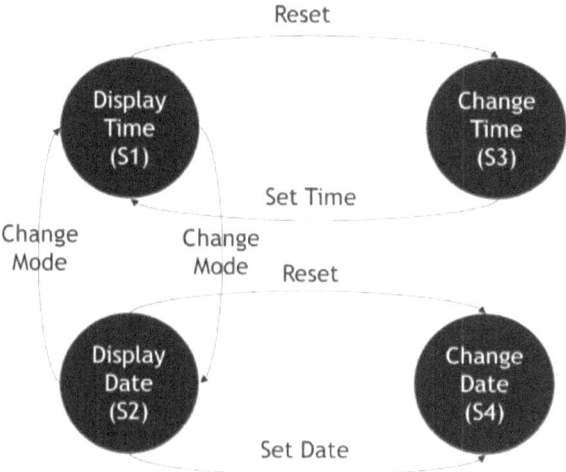

Determine the number of tests necessary to thoroughly examine all the invalid transactions as depicted in the provided state transition diagram.

A. 10 tests.
B. 6 tests.
C. 9 tests.
D. 16 tests.

29. Your team is working on a new feature for a software application. You have a user story with defined acceptance criteria. In line with ATDD practices, you decide to conduct a specification workshop. In this workshop, the user story and its acceptance criteria are analysed, discussed, and written by team members, including customers, developers, and testers. The next step involves creating test cases based on these acceptance criteria.

As per ATDD practices, what should be your approach immediately following the specification workshop?

A. Start implementing the user story and then develop test cases based on initial results.

B. Develop positive test cases confirming the correct behaviour without exceptions or error conditions.

C. Focus on creating test automation frameworks before developing any test cases.

D. Only develop negative test cases to ensure robust error handling in the application.

30. In an iterative software development process, what role do testers typically play during iteration planning?
    A. Testers are responsible for writing code for user stories.
    B. Testers primarily focus on risk analysis for user stories.
    C. Testers estimate development effort for the entire iteration.
    D. Testers break down user stories into tasks, specifically testing tasks.

31. Among the following options, which one represents an example of exit criteria in software testing?
    A. Availability of test data and resources.
    B. Completion of planned tests.
    C. Availability of testable requirements.
    D. Definition of Ready in Agile development.

32. In the testing quadrants model, which quadrant primarily contains non-functional tests, such as performance testing, and is often automated?
    A. Quadrant Q1 (technology facing, support the team)
    B. Quadrant Q2 (business facing, support the team)
    C. Quadrant Q3 (business facing, critique the product)
    D. Quadrant Q4 (technology facing, critique the product)

33. When responding to analysed product risks in the testing context, which action can be taken to mitigate these risks, demonstrating a proactive approach to improving the overall testing process?

A. Utilising automated testing tools exclusively for all types of testing.
B. Escalating all risks to senior management for resolution.
C. Implementing a comprehensive test coverage matrix for all quality characteristics.
D. Selecting testers with the right experience and skills suitable for the identified risk type.

34. As a test manager in a globally distributed software development team, you must effectively communicate the ongoing status of testing activities. Considering the geographical distance and time differences among team members, which of the following methods would be most appropriate to ensure clear and effective communication of the testing status?
    A. Relying solely on verbal communication during occasional team meetings.
    B. Utilizing dashboards and formal test reports to provide real-time updates and detailed analysis.
    C. Using only online documentation without any additional communication channels.
    D. Send personal emails with updates to individual team members.

35. As a test manager, you oversee a project involving frequent updates to both the software and test cases. To maintain the integrity and effectiveness of the testing process, you decide to implement configuration management (CM). Which of the following actions best illustrates the role of CM in supporting your testing activities?
    A. Schedule team meetings regularly to discuss the progress of testing.
    B. Ensuring all test items, including test cases and scripts, are uniquely identified, version-controlled, and tracked for changes.
    C. Focusing solely on automating test case execution without tracking their versions or changes.

D. Only documenting test results without keeping a record of the test cases and scripts used.

36. You are managing a testing project, and your team has estimated the test effort for a specific testing phase using the three-point estimation technique. The estimations provided are as follows:
    - Most Optimistic Estimate (a): 8 person-days
    - Most Likely Estimate (m): 14 person-days
    - Most Pessimistic Estimate (b): 22 person-days

    Calculate the Standard Deviation (SD) for the test effort estimation in this scenario.
    A. 2 person-days
    B. 4 person-days
    C. 6 person-days
    D. 8 person-days

37. You are the test manager for a complex software project with interdependent test cases, and you need to create a test execution sequence based on the priority of test cases and their dependencies. The project has identified five critical test cases, each with its own priority and dependencies on other test cases. Your goal is determining which test case should be executed in the third position, considering both priority and dependencies.

    Here are the five test cases, along with their priorities and dependencies:
    - Test Case X (Priority: High, Dependencies: None)
    - Test Case Y (Priority: Medium, Dependencies: Test Case X)
    - Test Case Z (Priority: Low, Dependencies: Test Case Y)
    - Test Case W (Priority: High, Dependencies: None)
    - Test Case V (Priority: Medium, Dependencies: Test Case W)

In the prioritised execution sequence of the five test cases, considering both priority and dependencies, which test case should be executed in the third position?

A. Test Case X
B. Test Case Y
C. Test Case Z
D. Test Case W

38. You are a tester who has discovered a defect during dynamic software application testing. The defect causes the application to crash when a specific sequence of inputs is provided. You are preparing a defect report. Which of the following pieces of information is most crucial to include in your report to ensure that those responsible for resolving the defect have sufficient information?

    A. A suggestion for a new feature that could prevent similar defects in the future.
    B. The sequence of inputs provided, the expected behaviour, and the actual behaviour observed, including details of the application crash.
    C. The financial impact assessment of the defect on the company's revenue.
    D. The history of all changes made in the application over the last month.

39. Which of the following test tools is primarily used to increase the efficiency of the test process by facilitating the management of the Software Development Life Cycle, requirements, tests, defects, and configuration?

    A. Static testing tools
    B. Management tools
    C. Test execution and coverage tools
    D. Non-functional testing tools

40. Which of the following is a potential risk associated with using test automation in software testing?
    A. Increased efficiency in manual testing processes
    B. Dependency on a tool vendor which may go out of business or provide poor support
    C. Reduced need for human critical thinking in the testing process
    D. Enhanced compatibility with all development platforms

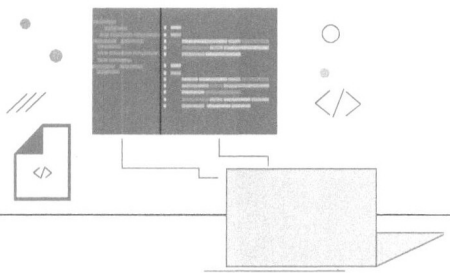

CHAPTER Y

ANSWERS TO SAMPLE EXAM

Question No	Answer	LO	Justification
1	B	FL-1.1.1 (K1)	Testing is necessary not only to ensure the quality of the software but also to meet contractual or legal requirements and comply with regulatory standards. While option A mentions involving users, it's not the primary purpose of testing, and it can be challenging and costly to involve a representative set of users in the development project. Option C is incorrect because testing and debugging are separate activities. Option D is also incorrect because testing while contributing to project management decisions, does not replace project management activities.
2	D	FL-1.5.2 (K1)	The whole Team approach increases collaboration between the Test team and business representatives. It also improves communication and team dynamics. Team members can benefit from the skill set present within the team.

3	B	FL-1.2.1 (K2)	While people often use the terms "testing" and "quality assurance" (QA) interchangeably, testing and QA are not the same. Testing is a form of quality control (QC).
4	D	FL-1.3.1 (K2)	We have to distribute testing efforts according to the complexity of the module. Testing should be more focused on the module which has more defects.
5	B	FL-1.4.1 (K2)	Actual test results are compared with the expected results as the main activity during test execution.
6	D	FL-1.4.2 (K2)	The revised question requires a more nuanced understanding of how different contextual factors shape the test process. The correct answer, D, reflects the complexity of these interactions and the fact that no single factor can be isolated as the predominant influencer. This aligns with the provided content, which emphasises the multifaceted nature of the impact of various contextual factors on testing decisions. The other options are partially correct but fail to encapsulate the comprehensive influence of all the mentioned contextual factors.

Answers to Sample Exam

| 7 | B | FL-1.4.4 (K2) | Option A is incorrect because the test cases do not calculate residual risk; they are linked to requirements for coverage assessment. Residual risk evaluation is derived from the test results associated with identified risks.
Option C is inaccurate as it oversimplifies the relationship between test cases and test results, ignoring the crucial role of risk assessment and requirement coverage.
Option D is incorrect as it understates the role of traceability, which is essential not just for defect reporting but also for requirement coverage and risk assessment. Therefore, option B is the most accurate, encompassing the key aspects of traceability in software testing. |

8	B	FL-1.5.3 (K2)	Ideally, we want close collaboration between testers and developers, which is not increased by isolation. Thus, this is a disadvantage Testers and developers have varied backgrounds, technical viewpoints, and potential biases, allowing testers to usefully challenge assumptions made by stakeholders during system specification and implementation. Thus, this is an advantage The main disadvantage of independence in testing is that testers may become isolated from the development team, leading to communication problems, a lack of collaboration, and potentially an adversarial relationship, with testers being blamed for delays and bottlenecks in the release process. Thus, this is a disadvantage One of the disadvantages of independence in testing is that testers may become isolated from the development team, leading to developers feeling less accountable for quality. Thus, this is a disadvantage The primary benefit of independence in testing is that testers are more likely to identify different types of failures and defects compared to developers, due to their varied backgrounds, technical viewpoints, and potential biases, including cognitive bias

Answers to Sample Exam

9	B	FL-2.1.2 (K1)	Every software development activity has a corresponding test activity. Different test levels have specific and different test objectives, allowing testing to be appropriately comprehensive while avoiding redundancy. Testing should apply the principle of early testing.
10	C	FL-2.1.3 (K1)	TDD, ATDD and BDD are similar development approaches apply the principle of early testing and follows a shift-left approach. The tests are defined before the code is written.
11	B	FL-2.2.1 (K2)	Test reports, test cases and test plans do not distinguish the test levels.
12	B	FL-2.2.3 (K2)	The correct answer differentiates the two types of testing based on their specific objectives. Confirmation testing is conducted to ensure that a specific defect that was previously identified has been successfully rectified. This often involves re-running the tests that failed initially due to the defect. On the other hand, regression testing is broader in scope and aims to ascertain that recent changes, including defect fixes, have not introduced new errors or adversely impacted existing functionalities of the system. This distinction aligns with the provided content, which clearly outlines the purposes and methods of both confirmation and regression testing.

13	D	FL-2.1.1 (K2)	The correct answer reflects the nuances of how different SDLC models affect the testing process. In sequential models like Waterfall, dynamic testing is more common in the later phases due to the nature of the development process. In contrast, iterative and incremental models, including Agile, facilitate early and continuous testing (both static and dynamic) due to frequent iterations and the emphasis on adaptability. Agile, in particular, focuses on lightweight documentation and extensive test automation to accommodate frequent changes. This option aligns with the provided content, which details these differences in approach to testing based on the SDLC model.
14	C	FL-2.1.5 (K2)	A shift-left approach might result in extra training, effort, and/or costs earlier in the process, but it is expected to save effort and/or costs later in the process. For the shift-left approach, it is important that stakeholders are convinced and bought into this concept.

15	C	FL-3.1.1 (K1)	The correct answer, according to the provided content, is third-party executable code that is legally restricted from analysis. This type of work product is unsuitable for static testing as it is difficult to interpret by human beings and should not be analysed by tools for legal reasons. The other options, such as requirement specification documents, test cases, test plans, and source code, are all appropriate for static testing as they can be read, and understood, and have a structure against which they can be checked.
16	C	FL-3.2.3 (K1)	The role responsible for ensuring the effective running of review meetings, including mediation, time management, and creating a safe review environment for open discussions, is the Moderator (also known as the Facilitator). This role is crucial in maintaining a productive and collaborative atmosphere during reviews. The other roles have different responsibilities, such as the Manager deciding what to review and provide resources, the Author creating and fixing the work product, the Scribe collating anomalies and recording review information, and the Reviewer performing the actual reviews.

17	B	FL-3.1.2 (K2)	The correct answer reflects the key benefits of static testing as outlined in the provided content. Static testing allows for early defect detection in the SDLC, including issues that might not be caught by dynamic testing, such as unreachable code or problems in non-executable work products. It also fosters improved communication among stakeholders and helps build a shared understanding of the project requirements. Moreover, static testing can lead to lower overall project costs due to reduced time and effort in fixing defects later in the project. The other options do not accurately represent the value of static testing in the SDLC.
18	D	FL-3.2.4 (K2)	Inspections are the most formal type of review and follow a complete generic process. Their main objective is to find the maximum number of anomalies. Additionally, inspections collect metrics for process improvement. In contrast, informal reviews do not follow a defined process and do not require formal documented output. Walkthroughs serve various objectives, including educating reviewers and gaining consensus. Technical reviews are led by a moderator and involve technically qualified reviewers, focusing on technical problem-solving and anomaly detection.

19	C	FL-4.1.1 (K2)	Black-box testing, also known as specification-based testing, relies on an analysis of the specified behaviour of the test object without referencing its internal structure. Test cases generated using black-box testing are independent of how the software is implemented. This means that even if the software's implementation changes while the required behaviour remains the same, the same test cases can still be useful.
20	B	FL-4.3.2 (K2)	The primary goal of branch testing is to design test cases that exercise branches in the code until an acceptable level of coverage is achieved. Coverage is measured as the number of branches exercised by the test cases divided by the total number of branches, expressed as a percentage. Achieving 100% branch coverage ensures that all branches in the code, both unconditional and conditional, are exercised.
21	C	FL-4.3.3 (K2)	The false statement is that white-box testing relies solely on the software specification for defect detection. In reality, white-box testing considers the entire software implementation, including internal logic and code structure, and is not solely reliant on the software specification. Black-box testing uses the software specification/requirements.

22	C	FL-4.4.1 (K2)	While boundary value analysis and equivalence partitioning are valuable black box testing techniques, they may not specifically target a "divide by zero" error unless the requirement explicitly states so. Error guessing, on the other hand, is a test technique that relies on the tester's knowledge and experience to anticipate errors and defects, including the "divide by zero" error, based on explicit requirements and common knowledge about potential software issues.
23	A	FL-4.4.2 (K2)	Exploratory testing is characterised by its unscripted and dynamic nature, where testers do not follow predefined test cases and steps. Instead, they explore the software while simultaneously designing, executing, and evaluating tests. This differentiates it from traditional scripted testing methods.
24	C	FL-4.5.2 (K2)	Scenario-oriented acceptance criteria in Behaviour-Driven Development (BDD) commonly follow the Given/When/Then structure. This format helps in defining the initial condition (Given), the action or event (When), and the expected outcome (Then).

25	A	FL-4.2.1 (K3)	In this simplified scenario, we have three distinct rules, each representing a separate partition of input data. The equivalence partitioning testing technique would divide these into: Exercise: 2 partitions (at least 150 minutes per week, less than 150 minutes) Health Check-ups: 2 partitions (undergoes annual check-up, does not undergo check-up) Alcohol Consumption: 2 partitions (non-drinker, drinker) This results in a total of 2 + 2 + 2 = 6 partitions. However, the minimum number of test cases needed to cover all these partitions is 2. This is because multiple partitions can be tested simultaneously (like exercising and undergoing health check-ups).
26	D	FL-4.2.2 (K3)	Two-point boundary value analysis focuses on the boundary values of the input domain. In this case, the boundary values are 15 and 25 degrees Celsius. The analysis should include tests that check the values just below and above the boundary, in addition to the boundary values. Therefore, the minimal set of tests should include: 14 degrees Celsius (just below the lower boundary) 15 degrees Celsius (lower boundary) 25 degrees Celsius (upper boundary) 26 degrees Celsius (just above the upper boundary)

27	B	FL-4.2.3 (K3)	Each column represents a unique combination of conditions in a decision table. For the RiskEvaluator application, we have the following conditions to consider: Age: Four options (under 18, 18 to 35, 36 to 65, over 65) Education: Three options (elementary or high school, undergraduate, graduate) Place of Residence: Two options (city, village) So, there will be a total of 4 x 3 x 2, which is 24 possible combinations/rules.
28	A	FL-4.2.4 (K3)	The total number of states here is: 4 (S1, S2, S3, S4) Total number of actions are: 4 (Change Mode, Set Time, Set Date, Reset) So, the total possible transitions are 4 x 4, which is 16. Out of which, 6 transitions are shown in the state transition diagram, which are valid, so the number of invalid transitions is 16 – 6, which is 10.
29	B	FL-4.5.3 (K3)	In ATDD, following the specification workshop where the user story and its acceptance criteria are defined, the next step is to create test cases based on these criteria. The first test cases typically developed are positive test cases, confirming the correct behaviour without exceptions or error conditions. This approach helps guide the team in implementing the user story correctly.

30	D	FL-5.1.2 (K1)	During iteration planning in iterative software development, testers play a crucial role in breaking down user stories into tasks, including defining the testing tasks required to successfully complete each user story. This helps ensure testing efforts are appropriately planned and executed within the iteration. While risk analysis and test effort estimation are important aspects and everyone should be involved, not just the testers, breaking down user stories into testing-specific tasks is the responsibility of testers during iteration planning.
31	B	FL-5.1.3 (K2)	Exit criteria in software testing define what must be achieved to declare an activity completed. This typically includes measures related to the thoroughness of testing, such as the completion of planned tests, achieved levels of coverage, and other relevant criteria. Option B correctly represents an example of exit criteria as it indicates the completion of planned tests.
32	D	FL-5.1.7 (K2)	In the testing quadrants model, Quadrant Q4 is characterised as "technology facing" and "critique the product." This quadrant primarily contains non-functional tests, except usability tests, and these tests are often automated. Quadrants Q1, Q2, and Q3 have different focuses and contain different types of tests, as described in the model.

33	D	FL-5.2.4 (K2)	Mitigating product risks by testing involves a proactive approach to risk reduction. One of the key actions is selecting testers with the right experience and skills suitable for the identified risk type. This ensures the testing team is well-equipped to address specific risks and contribute to risk mitigation. While potentially useful in testing, the other options do not directly address the proactive measures needed to mitigate identified product risks.
34	B	FL-5.3.3 (K2)	For a distributed team with limited face-to-face communication due to geographical distance or time differences, using dashboards and formal test reports is an effective way to communicate testing status. Dashboards, such as CI/CD dashboards, task boards, and burn-down charts, provide real-time updates and visual representations of progress. At the same time, formal test reports offer detailed analysis and documentation of testing activities. This combination ensures that all team members, regardless of location, can access current and comprehensive information about the testing status. The other options, while applicable in specific contexts, may not be as effective in a distributed team environment due to limitations in real-time communication, depth of information, or personalisation.

Answers to Sample Exam

35	B	FL-5.4.1 (K2)	Configuration management plays a crucial role in testing by providing a disciplined approach to identifying, controlling, and tracking test-related work products. This includes ensuring that all test items, such as test cases and scripts, are uniquely identified, version-controlled, and tracked for changes. This practice helps maintain traceability and integrity throughout the testing process, essential for testing effectiveness, especially in projects with frequent updates. The other options, while relevant to general project management or testing practices, do not directly illustrate the specific role of configuration management in supporting testing activities.
36	A	FL-5.1.4 (K3)	To calculate the Standard Deviation (SD) in the three-point estimation technique, you can use the formula SD = (b - a) / 6. In this scenario, the values are a=8 and b=22. Plugging these values into the formula: SD = (22 - 8) / 6 = 14 / 6 = 2.33 (rounded to 2), making option B the correct answer.

| 37 | B | FL-5.1.5 (K3) | To determine the test case to be executed in the third position, we need to consider both priority and dependencies. Test Case X (High priority) and Test Case W (High priority) have no dependencies and can be executed first. Among the remaining test cases, Test Case Y (Medium priority) and Test Case V (Medium priority) are the next in priority order and depend on Test Case X and Test Case W, which are already executed. Therefore, either Test Case Y or Test Case V should be executed in the third position. Looking at the provided answers, Test Case V is not available, so Test Case Y should be the correct answer. |
| 38 | B | FL-5.5.1 (K3) | For effective defect management, particularly in dynamic testing, providing detailed information about the defect is crucial to enable its reproduction and resolution. This includes the specific sequence of inputs that led to the defect, the expected behaviour of the application under these conditions, and the actual observed behaviour, including details of the crash. This information is critical for developers or engineers responsible for fixing the defect, as it allows them to understand the context and nature of the issue. The other options, while potentially applicable in other contexts, are not as critical for the immediate purpose of resolving the specific defect. |

39	B	FL-6.1.1 (K2)	Management tools are designed to increase the efficiency of the test process. They do this by facilitating the management of various aspects of the Software Development Life Cycle (SDLC), including requirements, tests, defects, and configuration. This makes them distinct from other types of tools like static testing tools (which support reviews and static analysis), test execution and coverage tools (which facilitate automated test execution and coverage measurement), and non-functional testing tools (which are used for non-functional testing that is difficult or impossible to perform manually).
40	B	FL-6.2.1 (K1)	One of the risks of using test automation is the dependency on the tool vendor, which can be problematic if the vendor goes out of business, retires the tool, sells it to a different vendor, or provides inadequate support. This risk is significant as it can affect the sustainability and reliability of the testing process. The other options, such as increased efficiency in manual processes, reduced need for human critical thinking, and enhanced compatibility with all development platforms, do not accurately represent the potential risks associated with test automation.

Explore More with SAJO Academy

www.sajoacademy.com

www.ingramcontent.com/pod-product-compliance
Lightning Source LLC
LaVergne TN
LVHW091634070526
838199LV00044B/1055